English / Portuguese
Inglês/Português

THE OXFORD

Picture Dictionary

NORMA SHAPIRO AND JAYME ADELSON-GOLDSTEIN

Translated by Cambridge Translation Resources, Inc.

Oxford University Press

Oxford University Press
198 Madison Avenue, New York, NY 10016 USA
Great Clarendon Street, Oxford OX2 6DP England

Oxford New York
Athens Auckland Bangkok Bogotá Buenos Aires
Calcutta Cape Town Chennai Dar es Salaam
Delhi Florence Hong Kong Istanbul Karachi
Kuala Lumpur Madrid Melbourne Mexico City
Mumbai Nairobi Paris São Paulo Singapore
Taipei Tokyo Toronto Warsaw

And associated companies in
Berlin Ibadan

OXFORD is a trademark of Oxford University Press.

Copyright © 1999 Oxford University Press

Library of Congress Cataloging-in-Publication Data

Shapiro, Norma.
      The Oxford picture dictionary. English-Brazilian
      Portuguese / Norma Shapiro and Jayme Adelson-
      Goldstein; translated by Cambridge Translation
      Resources, Inc.
          p.   cm.
      Includes bibliographical references and indexes.
      ISBN 0-19-436281-7
      1. English language—Dictionaries—Portuguese.
      2. Picture dictionaries, English.   3. Picture dictionaries,
      Portuguese.
        I. Adelson-Goldstein, Jayme. II. Title.
      PC5328.S53   1999   98-55453
      423'.69—dc21

No unauthorized photocopying.

Translation reviewed by Eliana Riva Campelo and
Ieda Yamasaki-Sousa
Editorial Manager: Susan Lanzano
Senior Editor: Eliza Jensen
Senior Production Editor: Robyn F. Clemente
Art Director: Lynn Luchetti
Senior Designer: Susan P. Brorein
Art Buyer: Tracy A. Hammond
Production Services by: Cambridge Translation Resources, Inc.
Production Manager: Abram Hall
Cover design by Silver Editions

Printing (last digit): 10 9 8 7 6 5 4 3 2

Printed in Hong Kong.

Illustrations by: David Aikins, Doug Archer, Craig Attebery,
Garin Baker, Sally Bensusen, Eliot Bergman, Mark Bischel, Dan
Brown / Artworks NY, Roy Douglas Buchman, George Burgos /
Larry Dodge, Carl Cassler, Mary Chandler, Robert Crawford, Jim
Delapine, Judy Francis, Graphic Chart and Map Co., Dale
Gustafson, Biruta Akerbergs Hansen, Marcia Hartsock, C.M.I.,
David Hildebrand, The Ivy League of Artists, Inc. / Judy
Degraffenreid, The Ivy League of Artists, Inc. / Tom Powers, The
Ivy League of Artists, Inc. / John Rice, Pam Johnson, Ed
Kurtzman, Narda Lebo, Scott A. MacNeill / MACNEILL &
MACINTOSH, Andy Lendway / Deborah Wolfe Ltd., Jeffrey
Mangiat, Suzanne Mogensen, Mohammad Mansoor, Tom
Newsom, Melodye Benson Rosales, Stacey Schuett, Rob
Schuster, James Seward, Larry Taugher, Bill Thomson, Anna
Veltfort, Nina Wallace, Wendy Wassink-Ackison, Michael
Wepplo, Don Wieland
Thanks to Mike Mikos for his preliminary architectural sketches
of several pieces.

References
Boyer, Paul S., Clifford E. Clark, Jr., Joseph F. Kett, Thomas L.
Purvis, Harvard Sitkoff, Nancy Woloch *The Enduring Vision: A
History of the American People,* Lexington, Massachusetts:
D.C. Heath and Co., 1990.

Grun, Bernard, *The Timetables of History: A Horizontal Linkage
of People and Events,* (based on Werner Stein's Kulturfahrplan)
New York: A Touchstone Book, Simon and Schuster, 1946,
1963, 1975, 1979.

Statistical Abstract of the United States: 1996, 116th Edition,
Washington, DC: US Bureau of the Census, 1996.

The World Book Encyclopedia, Chicago: World Book Inc., a
Scott Fetzer Co., 1988 Edition.

Toff, Nancy, Editor-in-Chief, *The People of North America*
(Series), New York: Chelsea House Publishers, Main Line
Books, 1988.

Trager, James, *The People's Chronology, A Year-by-Year Record
of Human Events from Prehistory to the Present,* New York:
Henry Holt Reference Book, 1992.

Acknowledgments

The publisher and authors would like to thank the following people for reviewing the manuscript and/or participating in focus groups as the book was being developed:

Ana Maria Aguilera, Lubie Alatriste, Ann Albarelli, Margaret Albers, Sherry Allen, Fiona Armstrong, Ted Auerbach, Steve Austen, Jean Barlow, Sally Bates, Sharon Batson, Myra Baum, Mary Beauparlant, Gretchen Bitterlin, Margrajean Bonilla, Mike Bostwick, Shirley Brod, Lihn Brown, Trish Brys-Overeem, Lynn Bundy, Chris Bunn, Carol Carvel, Leslie Crucil, Jill DeLa Llata, Robert Denheim, Joshua Denk, Kay Devonshire, Thomas Dougherty, Gudrun Draper, Sara Eisen, Lynda Elkins, Ed Ende, Michele Epstein, Beth Fatemi, Andra R. Fawcett, Alice Fiedler, Harriet Fisher, James Fitzgerald, Mary Fitzsimmons, Scott Ford, Barbara Gaines, Elizabeth Garcia Grenados, Maria T. Gerdes, Penny Giacalone, Elliott Glazer, Jill Gluck de la Llata, Javier Gomez, Pura Gonzales, Carole Goodman, Joyce Grabowski, Maggie Grennan, Joanie Griffin, Sally Hansen, Fotini Haritos, Alice Hartley, Fernando Herrera, Ann Hillborn, Mary Hopkins, Lori Howard, Leann Howard, Pamela Howard, Rebecca Hubner, Jan Jarrell, Vicki Johnson, Michele Kagan, Nanette Kafka, Gena Katsaros, Evelyn Kay, Greg Keech, Cliff Ker, Gwen Kerner-Mayer, Marilou Kessler, Patty King, Linda Kiperman, Joyce Klapp, Susan Knutson, Sandy Kobrine, Marinna Kolaitis, Donna Korol, Lorraine Krampe, Karen Kuser, Andrea Lang, Nancy Lebow, Tay Lesley, Gale Lichter, Sandie Linn, Rosario Lorenzano, Louise Louie, Cheryl Lucas, Ronna Magy, Juanita Maltese, Mary Marquardsen, Carmen Marques Rivera, Susan McDowell, Alma McGee, Jerry McLeroy, Kevin McLure, Joan Meier, Patsy Mills, Judy Montague, Vicki Moore, Eneida Morales, Glenn Nadelbach, Elizabeth Neblett, Kathleen Newton, Yvonne Nishio, Afra Nobay, Rosa Elena Ochoa, Jean Owensby, Jim Park, John Perkins, Jane Pers, Laura Peskin, Maria Pick, Percy Pleasant, Selma Porter, Kathy Quinones, Susan Ritter, Martha Robledo, Maureen Rooney, Jean Rose, David Ross, Julietta Ruppert, Lorraine Ruston, Susan Ryan, Frederico Salas, Leslie Salmon, Jim Sandifer, Linda Sasser, Lisa Schreiber, Mary Segovia, Abe Shames, Debra Shaw, Stephanie Shipp, Pat Singh, Mary Sklavos, Donna Stark, Claire Cocoran Stehling, Lynn Sweeden, Joy Tesh, Sue Thompson, Christine Tierney, Laura Topete, Carmen Villanueva, Laura Webber, Renée Weiss, Beth Winningham, Cindy Wislofsky, Judy Wood, Paula Yerman.

A special thanks to Marna Shulberg and the students of the Saticoy Branch of Van Nuys Community Adult School.

We would also like to thank the following individuals and organizations who provided their expertise:

Carl Abato, Alan Goldman, Dr. Larry Falk, Caroll Gray, Henry Haskell, Susan Haskell, Los Angeles Fire Department, Malcolm Loeb, Barbara Lozano, Lorne Dubin, United Farm Workers.

Authors' Acknowledgments

Throughout our careers as English language teachers, we have found inspiration in many places—in the classroom with our remarkable students, at schools, conferences, and workshops with our fellow teachers, and with our colleagues at the ESL Teacher Institute. We are grateful to be part of this international community.

We would like to sincerely thank and acknowledge Eliza Jensen, the project's Senior Editor. Without Eliza, this book would not have been possible. Her indomitable spirit, commitment to clarity, and unwavering advocacy allowed us to realize the book we envisioned.

Creating this dictionary was a collaborative effort and it has been our privilege to work with an exceptionally talented group of individuals who, along with Eliza Jensen, make up the Oxford Picture Dictionary team. We deeply appreciate the contributions of the following people:

Lynn Luchetti, Art Director, whose aesthetic sense and sensibility guided the art direction of this book,

Susan Brorein, Senior Designer, who carefully considered the design of each and every page,

Klaus Jekeli, Production Editor, who pored over both manuscript and art to ensure consistency and accuracy, and

Tracy Hammond, Art Buyer, who skillfully managed thousands of pieces of art and reference material.

We also want to thank Susan Mazer, the talented artist who was by our side for the initial problem-solving and Mary Chandler who also lent her expertise to the project.

We have learned much working with Marjorie Fuchs, Lori Howard, and Renée Weiss, authors of the dictionary's ancillary materials. We thank them for their on-going contributions to the dictionary program.

We must make special mention of Susan Lanzano, Editorial Manager, whose invaluable advice, insights, and queries were an integral part of the writing process.

This book is dedicated to my husband, Neil Reichline, who has encouraged me to take the road less traveled, and to my sons, Eli and Alex, who have allowed me to sit at their baseball games with my yellow notepad. —NS

This book is lovingly dedicated to my husband, Gary and my daughter, Emily Rose, both of whom hugged me tight and let me work into the night. —JAG

A Letter to the Teacher

Welcome to The Oxford Picture Dictionary.

This comprehensive vocabulary resource provides you and your students with over 3,700 words, each defined by engaging art and presented in a meaningful context. *The Oxford Picture Dictionary* enables your students to learn and use English in all aspects of their daily lives. The 140 key topics cover home and family, the workplace, the community, health care, and academic studies. The topics are organized into 12 thematic units that are based on the curriculum of beginning and low-intermediate level English language coursework. The word lists of the dictionary include both single word entries and verb phrases. Many of the prepositions and adjectives are presented in phrases as well, demonstrating the natural use of words in conjunction with one another.

The Oxford Picture Dictionary uses a variety of visual formats, each suited to the topic being represented. Where appropriate, word lists are categorized and pages are divided into sections, allowing you to focus your students' attention on one aspect of a topic at a time.

Within the word lists:

- nouns, adjectives, prepositions, and adverbs are numbered,

- verbs are bolded and identified by letters, and

- targeted prepositions and adjectives within phrases are bolded.

The dictionary includes a variety of exercises and self access tools that will guide your students towards accurate and fluent use of the new words.

- Exercises at the bottom of the pages provide vocabulary development through pattern practice, application of the new language to other topics, and personalization questions.

- An alphabetical index assists students in locating all words and topics in the dictionary.

- A phonetic listing for each word in the index and a pronunciation guide give students the key to accurate pronunciation.

- A verb index of all the verbs presented in the dictionary provides students with information on the present, past, and past participle forms of the verbs.

The Oxford Picture Dictionary is the core of *The Oxford Picture Dictionary Program* which includes a *Dictionary Cassette,* a *Teacher's Book* and its companion *Focused Listening Cassette, Beginning* and *Intermediate Workbooks, Classic Classroom Activities* (a photocopiable activity book), *Overhead Transparencies,* and *Read All About It 1 and 2.* Bilingual editions of *The Oxford Picture Dictionary* are available in Spanish, Chinese, Vietnamese, and many other languages.

TEACHING THE VOCABULARY

Your students' needs and your own teaching philosophy will dictate how you use *The Oxford Picture Dictionary* with your students. The following general guidelines, however, may help you adapt the dictionary's pages to your particular course and students. (For topic-specific, step-by-step guidelines and activities for presenting and practicing the vocabulary on each dictionary page see the *Oxford Picture Dictionary Teacher's Book.*)

Preview the topic

A good way to begin any lesson is to talk with students to determine what they already know about the topic. Some different ways to do this are:

- Ask general questions related to the topic;

- Have students brainstorm a list of words they know from the topic; or

- Ask questions about the picture(s) on the page.

Present the vocabulary

Once you've discovered which words your students already know, you are ready to focus on presenting the words they need. Introducing 10–15 new words in a lesson allows students to really learn the new words. On pages where the word lists are longer, and students are unfamiliar with any of the words, you may wish to introduce the words by categories or sections, or simply choose the words you want in the lesson.

Here are four different presentation techniques. The techniques you choose will depend on the topic being studied and the level of your students.

- Say each new word and describe or define it within the context of the picture.

- Demonstrate verbs or verb sequences for the students, and have volunteers demonstrate the actions as you say them.

- Use Total Physical Response commands to build comprehension of the vocabulary: *Put the pencil on your book. Put it on your notebook. Put it on your desk.*

- Ask a series of questions to build comprehension and give students an opportunity to say the new words:

▶ Begin with *yes/no* questions. *Is #16 chalk?* (yes)

▶ Progress to *or* questions. *Is #16 chalk or a marker?* (chalk)

▶ Finally ask *Wh* questions.

What can I use to write on this paper? (a marker/ Use a marker.)

Check comprehension

Before moving on to the practice stage, it is helpful to be sure all students understand the target vocabulary. There are many different things you can do to check students' understanding. Here are two activities to try:

• Tell students to open their books and point to the items they hear you say. Call out target vocabulary at random as you walk around the room checking to see if students are pointing to the correct pictures.

• Make true/false statements about the target vocabulary. Have students hold up two fingers for true, three fingers for false. *You can write with a marker.* [two fingers] *You raise your notebook to talk to the teacher.* [three fingers]

Take a moment to review any words with which students are having difficulty before beginning the practice activities.

Practice the vocabulary

Guided practice activities give your students an opportunity to use the new vocabulary in meaningful communication. The exercises at the bottom of the pages are one source of guided practice activities.

• **Talk about...** This activity gives students an opportunity to practice the target vocabulary through sentence substitutions with meaningful topics.

   e.g. **Talk about your feelings.**

      I feel <u>happy</u> when I see my friends.

• **Practice...** This activity gives students practice using the vocabulary within common conversational functions such as making introductions, ordering food, making requests, etc.

   e.g. **Practice asking for things in the dining room.**

      Please pass <u>the platter</u>.

      May I have <u>the creamer</u>?

      Could I have <u>a fork</u>, please?

• **Use the new language.** This activity asks students to brainstorm words within various categories, or may

ask them to apply what they have learned to another topic in the dictionary. For example, on *Colors*, page 12, students are asked to look at *Clothing I*, pages 64–65, and name the colors of the clothing they see.

• **Share your answers.** These questions provide students with an opportunity to expand their use of the target vocabulary in personalized discussion. Students can ask and answer these questions in whole class discussions, pair or group work, or they can write the answers as journal entries.

Further guided and communicative practice can be found in the *Oxford Picture Dictionary Teacher's Book* and in *Classic Classroom Activities*. The *Oxford Picture Dictionary Beginning* and *Intermediate Workbooks* and the *Oxford Picture Dictionary Readers* provide your students with controlled and communicative reading and writing practice.

We encourage you to adapt the materials to suit the needs of your classes, and we welcome your comments and ideas. Write to us at:

Oxford University Press
ESL Department
198 Madison Avenue
New York, NY 10016

Jayme Adelson-Goldstein

Norma Shapiro

A Letter to the Student

Dear Student of English,

Welcome to *The Oxford Picture Dictionary.* The more than 3,700 words in this book will help you as you study English.

Each page in this dictionary teaches about a specific topic. The topics are grouped together in units. All pages in a unit have the same color and symbol. For example, each page in the Food unit has this symbol:

On each page you will see pictures and words. The pictures have numbers or letters that match the numbers or letters in the word lists. Verbs (action words) are identified by letters and all other words are identified by numbers.

How to find words in this book

- Use the Table of Contents, pages ix–xi.
  Look up the general topic you want to learn about.

- Use the Index, pages 173–205.
  Look up individual words in alphabetical (A–Z) order.

- Go topic by topic.
  Look through the book until you find something that interests you.

How to use the Index

When you look for a word in the index this is what you will see:

the word   the number (or letter) in the word list

apples [ăp/əlz] **50**–4

the pronunciation   the page number

If the word is on one of the maps, pages 122–125, you will find it in the Geographical Index on pages 206–208.

How to use the Verb Guide

When you want to know the past form of a verb or its past participle form, look up the verb in the verb guide. The regular verbs and their spelling changes are listed on pages 170–171. The simple form, past form, and past participle form of irregular verbs are listed on page 172.

Workbooks

There are two workbooks to help you practice the new words: *The Oxford Picture Dictionary Beginning* and *Intermediate Workbooks.*

As authors and teachers we both know how difficult English can be (and we're native speakers!). When we wrote this book, we asked teachers and students from the U.S. and other countries for their help and ideas. We hope their ideas and ours will help you. Please write to us with your comments or questions at:

Oxford University Press
ESL Department
198 Madison Avenue
New York, NY 10016

We wish you success!

Jayme Adelson-Goldstein   *Norma Shapiro*

Carta ao Estudante

Prezado estudante de inglês:

Bem-vindo ao *The Oxford Picture Dictionary*. As mais de 3.700 palavras neste livro o ajudarão a aprender inglês.

Cada página deste dicionário trata de um tópico específico. Os tópicos são agrupados em unidades e todas as páginas de uma unidade têm a mesma cor e o mesmo símbolo. Por exemplo, cada página da unidade sobre Alimentação apresenta o seguinte símbolo:

Em cada página você verá figuras e palavras. As figuras apresentam números ou letras que correspondem aos números ou às letras nas listas de palavras. Os verbos são identificados por letras e todas as outras palavras são identificadas por números.

Como encontrar palavras neste livro

- Use o Índice Temático, páginas ix-xi.
  Procure o tópico geral sobre o qual deseja aprender.

- Use o Índice Remissivo, páginas 173-205.
  Procure palavras específicas em ordem alfabética (A-Z)

- Procure tópico por tópico.
  Folheie o livro até encontrar algo que lhe interesse.

Como usar o Índice Remissivo

Ao procurar uma palavra no índice remissivo, você verá o seguinte:

a palavra   o número (ou a letra) na lista de palavra

apples [ăp/əlz] **50**—4

a pronúncia   o número da página

Se a palavra estiver em um dos mapas, nas páginas 122-125, você a encontrará no Índice Geográfico, nas páginas 206-208.

Como usar o Guia de Verbos

Quando desejar saber o passado ou particípio passado de um verbo, procure o verbo no Guia de Verbos. Os verbos regulares e as suas variações ortográficas estão listados nas páginas 170-171. O presente, passado e particípio passado dos verbos irregulares estão listados na página 172.

Livros de Exercício

Há dois livros de exercício para ajudá-lo a praticar as novas palavras:
O *The Oxford Picture Dictionary Beginning WorkBook* e o *Intermediate Workbook*.

Como autores e professores sabemos como pode ser difícil aprender inglês (e inglês é a nossa língua materna!). Quando elaboramos este livro, solicitamos a ajuda e as idéias de professores e estudantes dos Estados Unidos e de outros países. Esperamos que as idéias deles e as nossas ajudem vocês. Escreva-nos para fazer seus comentários ou para esclarecer dúvidas:

Oxford University Press
ESL Department
198 Madison Avenue
New York, NY 10016. - E.U.A

Boa sorte!

Jayme Adelson-Goldstein   *Norma Shapiro*

Contents   Índice temático

Contents   Índice temático

Índice temático   Contents

1. chalkboard
a lousa

2. screen
a tela

3. student
a estudante / a aluna

4. overhead projector
o retroprojetor

5. teacher
a professora

6. desk
a carteira

7. chair / seat
a cadeira

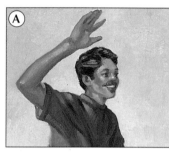

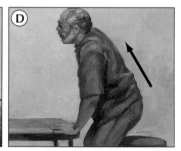

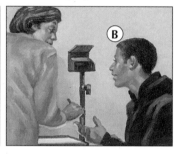

A. Raise your hand.
Levante a mão.

B. Talk to the teacher.
Fale com a professora.

C. Listen to a cassette.
Ouça uma fita cassete.

D. Stand up.
Levante-se.

E. Sit down. / Take a seat.
Sente-se.

F. Point to the picture.
Aponte para uma figura.

G. Write on the board.
Escreva na lousa.

H. Erase the board.
Apague a lousa.

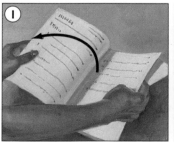

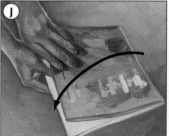

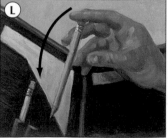

I. Open your book.
Abra o livro.

J. Close your book.
Feche o livro.

K. Take out your pencil.
Pegue o lápis.

L. Put away your pencil.
Guarde o lápis.

8. bookcase
a estante de livros

9. globe
o globo terrestre

10. clock
o relógio

11. cassette player
o toca-fitas

12. map
o mapa

13. pencil sharpener
o apontador de lápis

14. bulletin board
o quadro de avisos

15. computer
o computador

16. chalk
o giz

17. chalkboard eraser
o apagador

18. pen
a caneta

19. marker
a caneta hidrográfica /
o marcador de texto

20. pencil
o lápis

21. pencil eraser
a borracha

22. textbook
o livro

23. workbook
o caderno de exercícios

24. binder/notebook
o fichário

25. notebook paper
as folhas para fichário

26. spiral notebook
o caderno espiral

27. ruler
a régua

28. dictionary
o dicionário

29. picture dictionary
o dicionário ilustrado

30. the alphabet
o alfabeto

31. numbers
os números

Use the new language.

1. Name three things you can open.

2. Name three things you can put away.

3. Name three things you can write with.

Share your answers.

1. Do you like to raise your hand?

2. Do you ever listen to cassettes in class?

3. Do you ever write on the board?

Personal Information   Dados pessoais

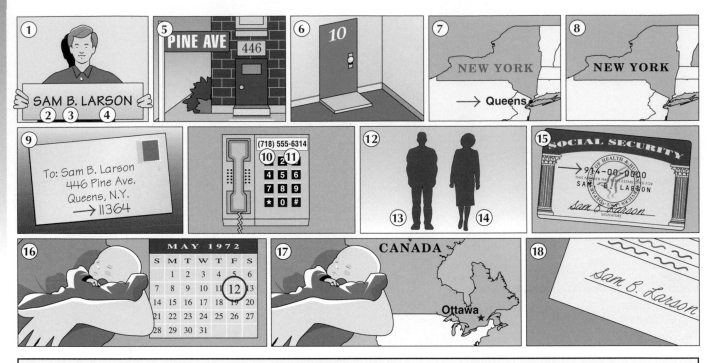

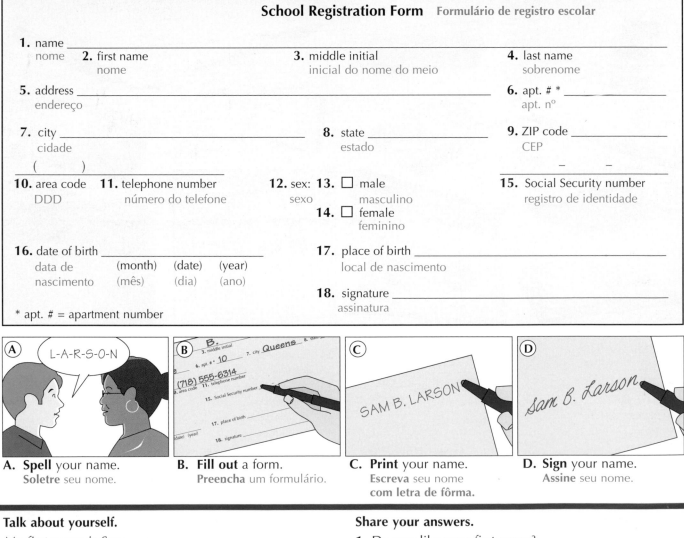

School Registration Form   Formulário de registro escolar

1. name _____
nome   **2.** first name   **3.** middle initial   **4.** last name
         nome   inicial do nome do meio   sobrenome

5. address _____   **6.** apt. # * _____
endereço   apt. nº

7. city _____   **8.** state _____   **9.** ZIP code _____
cidade   estado   CEP

(   ) _____   ___ – ___ – ___
10. area code   **11.** telephone number   **12.** sex: **13.** ☐ male   **15.** Social Security number
      DDD   número do telefone   sexo   masculino   registro de identidade

                                             14. ☐ female
                                                 feminino

16. date of birth _____   **17.** place of birth _____
    data de   (month)   (date)   (year)   local de nascimento
    nascimento   (mês)   (dia)   (ano)

                                                18. signature _____
                                                       assinatura

* apt. # = apartment number

A. **Spell** your name.
Soletre seu nome.

B. **Fill out** a form.
Preencha um formulário.

C. **Print** your name.
Escreva seu nome
com letra de fôrma.

D. **Sign** your name.
Assine seu nome.

Talk about yourself.

My first name is Sam.

My last name is spelled L-A-R-S-O-N.

I come from Ottawa.

Share your answers.

1. Do you like your first name?

2. Is your last name from your mother? father? husband?

3. What is your middle name?

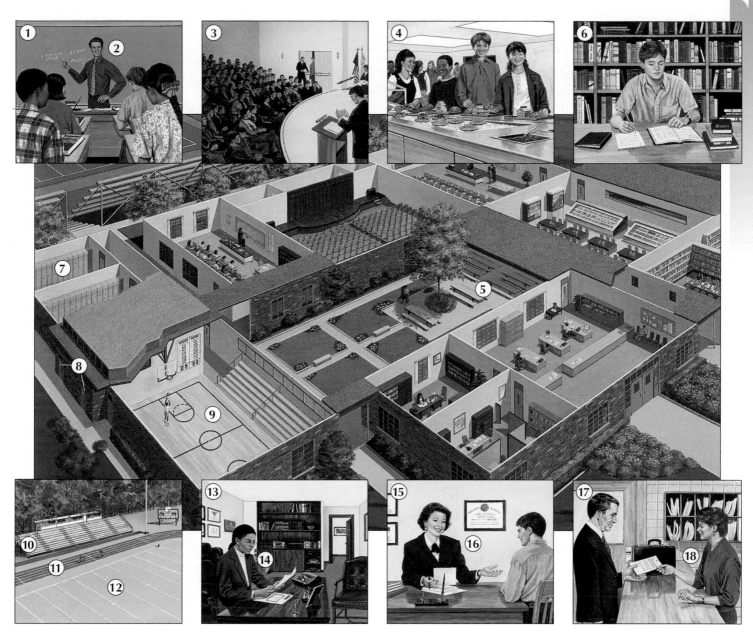

1. classroom a sala de aula	**7.** lockers os armários	**13.** principal's office a diretoria
2. teacher o professor	**8.** rest rooms os banheiros	**14.** principal a diretora
3. auditorium o auditório	**9.** gym o ginásio	**15.** counselor's office a sala da orientadora
4. cafeteria a lanchonete / o refeitório	**10.** bleachers a arquibancada	**16.** counselor a orientadora
5. lunch benches a mesa de refeição	**11.** track a pista de corrida / a pista de atletismo	**17.** main office a secretaria
6. library a biblioteca	**12.** field o campo	**18.** clerk a funcionária

More vocabulary

instructor: teacher

coach: gym teacher

administrator: principal or other school supervisor

Share your answers.

1. Do you ever talk to the principal of your school?

2. Is there a place for you to eat at your school?

3. Does your school look the same as or different from the one in the picture?

Dictionary work   Uso do dicionário

A. Look up a word.
Procure uma palavra.

B. Read the word.
Leia a palavra.

C. Say the word.
Fale a palavra.

D. Repeat the word.
Repita a palavra.

E. Spell the word.
Soletre a palavra.

F. Copy the word.
Copie a palavra.

Work with a partner   Trabalho com um colega

G. Ask a question.
Faça uma pergunta.

H. Answer a question.
Responda uma pergunta.

I. Share a book.
Compartilhe um livro.

J. Help your partner.
Ajude seu colega.

Work in a group   Trabalho em grupo

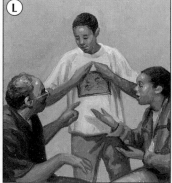

K. Brainstorm a list.
Elabore uma lista de idéias.

L. Discuss the list.
Discuta a lista de idéias.

M. Draw a picture.
Faça um desenho.

N. Dictate a sentence.
Dite uma frase.

Class work Trabalho em sala de aula

O. Pass out the papers.
Distribua as folhas.

P. Talk with each other.
Fale com os colegas.

Q. Collect the papers.
Recolha as folhas.

Follow directions Siga instruções

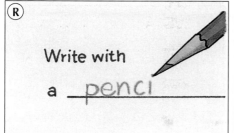

R. Fill in the blank.
Preencha a lacuna.

S. Circle the answer.
Circule a resposta.

T. Mark the answer sheet.
Marque a folha de respostas.

U. Cross out the word.
Risque a palavra.

V. Underline the word.
Sublinhe a palavra.

W. Put the words **in order.**
Coloque as palavras em **ordem.**

X. Match the items.
Faça a correspondência dos itens.

Y. Check your work.
Confira o que você escreveu.

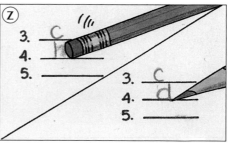

Z. Correct the mistake.
Corrija o erro.

Share your answers.

1. Do you like to work in groups?

2. Do you like to share books?

3. Do you like to answer questions?

4. Is it easy for you to talk with your classmates?

5. Do you always check your work?

6. Do you cross out your mistakes or erase them?

Everyday Conversation Conversa do dia-a-dia

A. greet someone
cumprimentar alguém

B. begin a conversation
iniciar uma conversa

C. end the conversation
encerrar uma conversa

D. introduce yourself
apresentar-se

E. make sure you **understand**
confirmar se você **entendeu**

F. introduce your friend
apresentar seu amigo

G. compliment your friend
elogiar sua amiga

H. thank your friend
agradecer a sua amiga

I. apologize
desculpar-se

Practice introductions.

Hi, I'm Sam Jones and this is my friend, Pat Green.

Nice to meet you. I'm Tomas Garcia.

Practice giving compliments.

That's a great sweater, Tomas.

Thanks, Pat. I like your shoes.

Look at **Clothing I,** pages **64–65** for more ideas.

1. telephone / phone
   o telefone

2. receiver
   o fone

3. cord
   o fio

4. local call
   a chamada local

5. long-distance call
   a chamada interurbana

6. international call
   a chamada internacional

7. operator
   o telefonista

8. directory assistance (411)
   auxílio à lista

9. emergency service (911)
   serviço de emergência

10. phone card
    o cartão telefônico

11. pay phone
    o telefone público

12. cordless phone
    o telefone sem fio

13. cellular phone
    o telefone celular

14. answering machine
    a secretária eletrônica

15. telephone book
    a lista telefônica

16. pager
    o pager

Using a pay phone   Usando o telefone público

A. **Pick up** the receiver.
   Tire o fone do gancho.

B. **Listen** for the dial tone.
   Espere dar linha.

C. **Deposit** coins.
   Coloque as moedas.

D. **Dial** the number.
   Disque o número.

E. **Leave** a message.
   Deixe um recado.

F. **Hang up** the receiver.
   Coloque o fone no gancho.

More vocabulary

When you get a person or place that you didn't want to call, we say you have the **wrong number.**

Share your answers.

1. What kinds of calls do you make?
2. How much does it cost to call your country?
3. Do you like to talk on the telephone?

Weather   O tempo

Temperature
Temperatura

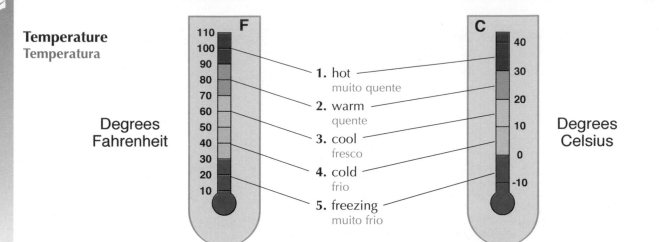

Degrees
Fahrenheit

Degrees
Celsius

1. hot
muito quente

2. warm
quente

3. cool
fresco

4. cold
frio

5. freezing
muito frio

6. sunny / clear
ensolarado / sem nuvens

7. cloudy
nublado

8. raining
chovendo

9. snowing
nevando

10. windy
ventando

11. foggy
enevoado / com neblina

12. humid
úmido

13. icy
coberto de gelo

14. smoggy
poluído e enevoado

15. heat wave
a onda de calor

16. thunderstorm
a tempestade

17. lightning
o relâmpago / o raio

18. hailstorm
a tempestade de granizo /
a chuva de pedras

19. hail
o granizo

20. snowstorm
a tempestade de neve

21. dust storm
a tempestade de poeira

Language note: *it is, there is*

For **1–14** we use,   *It's <u>cloudy</u>.*

For **15–21** we use,   *There's <u>a heat wave</u>.*
There's <u>lightning</u>.

Talk about the weather.

Today it's <u>hot</u>. It's <u>98 degrees</u>.
Yesterday it was <u>warm</u>. It was <u>85 degrees</u>.

1. **little** hand
   a mão **pequena**
2. **big** hand
   a mão **grande**

3. **fast** driver
   o motorista **veloz**
4. **slow** driver
   o motorista **lento**

5. **hard** chair
   a cadeira **dura**
6. **soft** chair
   a cadeira **macia**

7. **thick** book /
   fat book
   o livro **grosso** /
   espesso
8. **thin** book
   o livro **fino**

9. **full** glass
   o copo **cheio**
10. **empty** glass
    o copo **vazio**

11. **noisy** children /
    loud children
    as crianças **barulhentas**
12. **quiet** children
    as crianças **quietas**

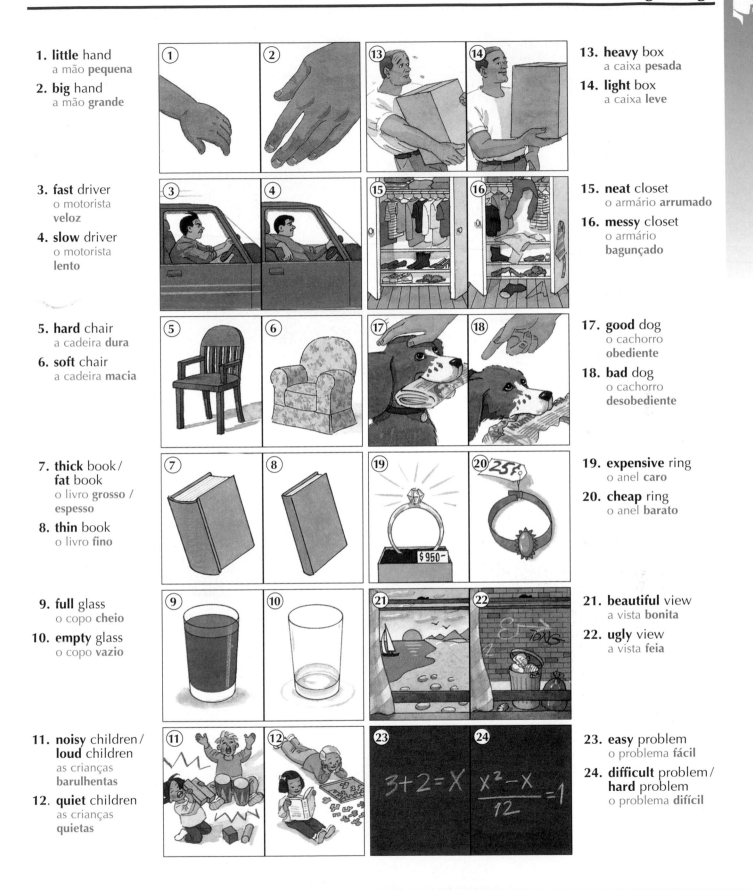

13. **heavy** box
    a caixa **pesada**
14. **light** box
    a caixa **leve**

15. **neat** closet
    o armário **arrumado**
16. **messy** closet
    o armário **bagunçado**

17. **good** dog
    o cachorro **obediente**
18. **bad** dog
    o cachorro **desobediente**

19. **expensive** ring
    o anel **caro**
20. **cheap** ring
    o anel **barato**

21. **beautiful** view
    a vista **bonita**
22. **ugly** view
    a vista **feia**

23. **easy** problem
    o problema **fácil**
24. **difficult** problem /
    hard problem
    o problema **difícil**

Use the new language.
1. Name three things that are thick.
2. Name three things that are soft.
3. Name three things that are heavy.

Share your answers.
1. Are you a slow driver or a fast driver?
2. Do you have a neat closet or a messy closet?
3. Do you like loud or quiet parties?

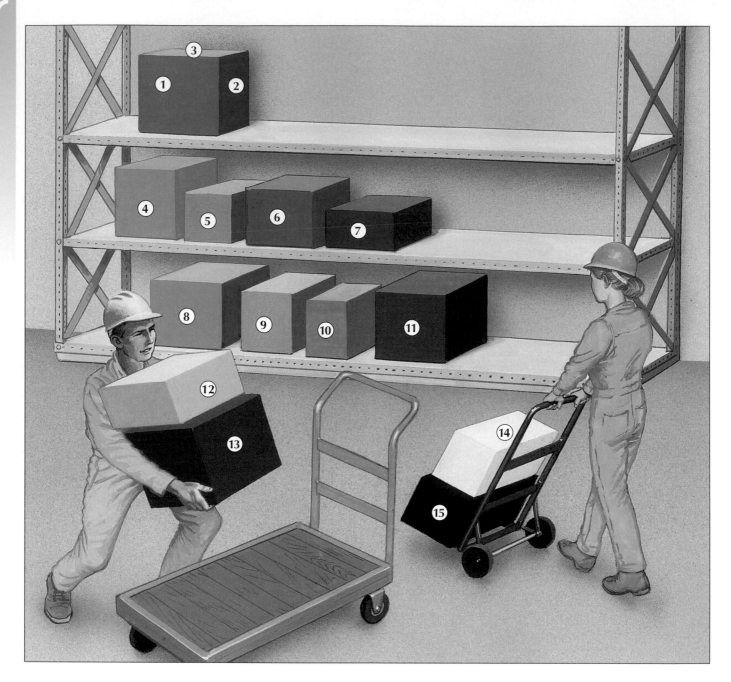

1. blue azul	6. orange laranja	11. brown marrom
2. dark blue azul-escuro	7. purple roxo	12. yellow amarelo
3. light blue azul-claro	8. green verde	13. red vermelho
4. turquoise azul-turquesa	9. beige bege	14. white branco
5. gray cinza	10. pink rosa	15. black preto

Use the new language.

Look at **Clothing I,** pages **64–65.**

Name the colors of the clothing you see.

That's <u>a dark blue suit</u>.

Share your answers.

1. What colors are you wearing today?

2. What colors do you like?

3. Is there a color you don't like? What is it?

1. The red box is **next to** the yellow box, **on the left.**
   A caixa vermelha está **ao lado da** caixa amarela, **à esquerda**.

2. The yellow box is **next to** the red box, **on the right.**
   A caixa amarela está **ao lado da** caixa vermelha, **à direita**.

3. The turquoise box is **behind** the gray box.
   A caixa azul-turquesa está **atrás da** caixa cinza.

4. The gray box is **in front of** the turquoise box.
   A caixa cinza está **na frente da** caixa azul-turquesa.

5. The dark blue box is **in** the beige box.
   A caixa azul-escura está **dentro da** caixa bege.

6. The green box is **above** the orange box.
   A caixa verde está **acima da** caixa laranja.

7. The orange box is **below** the green box.
   A caixa laranja está **abaixo da** caixa verde.

8. The white box is **on** the black box.
   A caixa branca está **sobre** a caixa preta.

9. The black box is **under** the white box.
   A caixa preta está **sob** a caixa branca.

10. The pink box is **between** the purple box and the brown box.
    A caixa rosa está **entre** a caixa roxa e a caixa marrom.

More vocabulary

near: in the same area
*The white box is **near** the black box.*

far from: not near
*The red box is **far from** the black box.*

HOME	1 8
VISITOR	2 2

SAN DIEGO 235 miles

Cardinals   Números cardinais

0	zero / zero	11	eleven / onze	21	twenty-one / vinte e um	101	one hundred one / cento e um
1	one / um	12	twelve / doze	22	twenty-two / vinte e dois	1,000	one thousand / mil
2	two / dois	13	thirteen / treze	30	thirty / trinta	1,001	one thousand one / mil e um
3	three / três	14	fourteen / quatorze	40	forty / quarenta	10,000	ten thousand / dez mil
4	four / quatro	15	fifteen / quinze	50	fifty / cinqüenta	100,000	one hundred thousand / cem mil
5	five / cinco	16	sixteen / dezesseis	60	sixty / sessenta	1,000,000	one million / um milhão
6	six / seis	17	seventeen / dezessete	70	seventy / setenta	1,000,000,000	one billion / um bilhão
7	seven / sete	18	eighteen / dezoito	80	eighty / oitenta		
8	eight / oito	19	nineteen / dezenove	90	ninety / noventa		
9	nine / nove	20	twenty / vinte	100	one hundred / cem		
10	ten / dez						

Ordinals   Números ordinais

1st	first / 1º primeiro	8th	eighth / 8º oitavo	15th	fifteenth / 15º décimo quinto
2nd	second / 2º segundo	9th	ninth / 9º nono	16th	sixteenth / 16º décimo sexto
3rd	third / 3º terceiro	10th	tenth / 10º décimo	17th	seventeenth / 17º décimo sétimo
4th	fourth / 4º quarto	11th	eleventh / 11º décimo primeiro	18th	eighteenth / 18º décimo oitavo
5th	fifth / 5º quinto	12th	twelfth / 12º décimo segundo	19th	nineteenth / 19º décimo nono
6th	sixth / 6º sexto	13th	thirteenth / 13º décimo terceiro	20th	twentieth / 20º vigésimo
7th	seventh / 7º sétimo	14th	fourteenth / 14º décimo quarto		

Roman numerals   Algarismos romanos

I	= 1	VII	= 7	XXX	= 30
II	= 2	VIII	= 8	XL	= 40
III	= 3	IX	= 9	L	= 50
IV	= 4	X	= 10	C	= 100
V	= 5	XV	= 15	D	= 500
VI	= 6	XX	= 20	M	= 1,000

Fractions Frações

1. 1/8 one-eighth
um oitavo

2. 1/4 one-fourth
um quarto

3. 1/3 one-third
um terço

4. 1/2 one-half
meio

5. 3/4 three-fourths
três quartos

6. 1 whole
inteiro

1 cup
3/4
2/3
1/2
1/3
1/4

Percents Porcentagens

7. 10% ten percent
10% dez por cento

8. 20% twenty percent
20% vinte por cento

9. 50% fifty percent
50% cinqüenta por cento

10. 80% eighty percent
80% oitenta por cento

11. 100% one hundred percent
100% cem por cento

Measurement Medidas

12. centimeter [cm]
centímetro [cm]

13. inch [in.]
polegada [pol.]

Equivalencies Equivalências

1 inch = 2.54 centimeters
1 yard = .91 meters
1 mile = 1.6 kilometers

12 inches = 1 foot
3 feet = 1 yard
1,760 yards = 1 mile

Dimensions Dimensões

14. height
altura

16. length
comprimento

15. depth
profundidade

17. width
largura

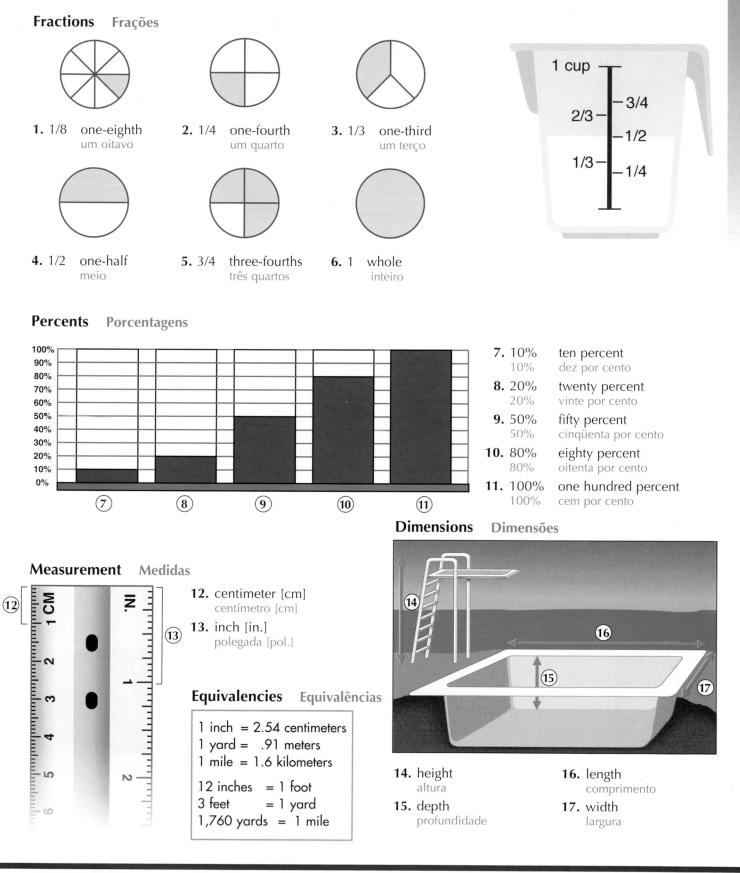

More vocabulary

measure: to find the size or amount of something

count: to find the total number of something

Share your answers.

1. How many students are in class today?

2. Who was the first person in class today?

3. How far is it from your home to your school?

Time Horas

1. second
segundo

2. minute   **3. hour**
minuto   hora

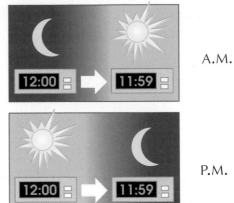

A.M.

P.M.

4. 1:00
one o'clock
uma hora

5. 1:05
one-oh-five
uma e cinco
five after one
uma e cinco

6. 1:10
one-ten
uma e dez
ten after one
uma e dez

7. 1:15
one-fifteen
uma e quinze
a quarter after one
uma e quinze

8. 1:20
one-twenty
uma e vinte
twenty after one
uma e vinte

9. 1:25
one twenty-five
uma e vinte e cinco
twenty-five after one
uma e vinte e cinco

10. 1:30
one-thirty
uma e trinta
half past one
uma e meia

11. 1:35
one thirty-five
uma e trinta e cinco
twenty-five to two
vinte e cinco para as duas

12. 1:40
one-forty
uma e quarenta
twenty to two
vinte para as duas

13. 1:45
one forty-five
uma e quarenta e cinco
a quarter to two
quinze para as duas

14. 1:50
one-fifty
uma e cinqüenta
ten to two
dez para as duas

15. 1:55
one fifty-five
uma e cinqüenta e cinco
five to two
cinco para as duas

Talk about the time.

What time is it? It's <u>10:00 a.m.</u>

What time do you wake up on weekdays? At <u>6:30 a.m.</u>

What time do you wake up on weekends? At <u>9:30 a.m.</u>

Share your answers.

1. How many hours a day do you study English?

2. You are meeting friends at 1:00. How long will you wait for them if they are late?

16. morning
a manhã

17. noon
o meio-dia

18. afternoon
a tarde

19. evening
o anoitecer

20. night
a noite

21. midnight
a meia-noite

22. early
adiantado / cedo

23. late
atrasado / tarde

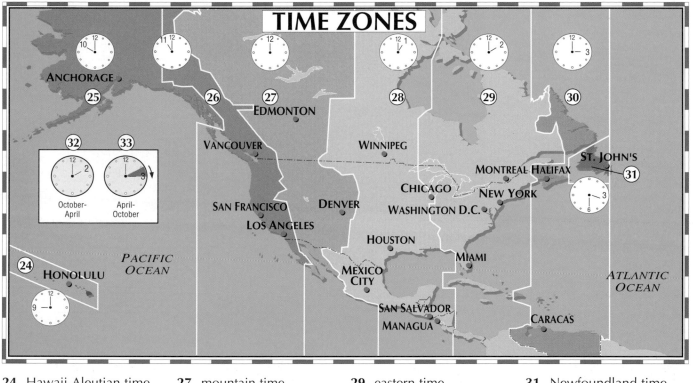

TIME ZONES

24. Hawaii-Aleutian time
horário do Havaí

25. Alaska time
horário do Alasca

26. Pacific time
horário da Costa do
Pacífico (EUA)

27. mountain time
horário da Região das
Montanhas Rochosas
(EUA)

28. central time
horário da Região Central
(EUA)

29. eastern time
horário da Região Leste
(EUA)

30. Atlantic time
horário do Atlântico
(EUA)

31. Newfoundland time
horário da Terra-Nova

32. standard time
horário padrão

33. daylight saving time
horário de verão

More vocabulary

on time: not early and not late

*He's **on time.***

Share your answers.

1. When do you watch television? study?
do housework?

2. Do you come to class on time? early? late?

Days of the week
Dias da semana

1. Sunday
   domingo
2. Monday
   segunda-feira
3. Tuesday
   terça-feira
4. Wednesday
   quarta-feira
5. Thursday
   quinta-feira
6. Friday
   sexta-feira
7. Saturday
   sábado
8. year
   o ano
9. month
   o mês
10. day
    o dia
11. week
    a semana
12. weekdays
    os dias da semana
13. weekend
    o fim de semana
14. date
    a data
15. today
    hoje
16. tomorrow
    amanhã
17. yesterday
    ontem
18. last week
    a semana passada
19. this week
    esta semana
20. next week
    a semana que vem
21. every day
    todos os dias
22. once a week
    uma vez por semana
23. twice a week
    duas vezes por semana
24. three times a week
    três vezes por semana

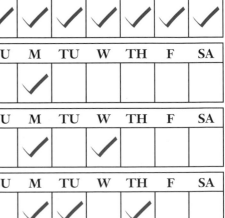

Talk about the calendar.

What's today's date? It's <u>March 10th</u>.

What day is it? It's <u>Tuesday</u>.

What day was yesterday? It was <u>Monday</u>.

Share your answers.

1. How often do you come to school?
2. How long have you been in this school?

2001

JAN ㉕						
SUN	MON	TUE	WED	THU	FRI	SAT
	1	2	3	4	5	6
7	8	9	10	11	12	13
14	15	16	17	18	19	20
21	22	23	24	25	26	27
28	29	30	31			

FEB ㉖						
SUN	MON	TUE	WED	THU	FRI	SAT
				1	2	3
4	5	6	7	8	9	10
11	12	13	14	15	16	17
18	19	20	21	22	23	24
25	26	27	28			

MAR ㉗						
SUN	MON	TUE	WED	THU	FRI	SAT
				1	2	3
4	5	6	7	8	9	10
11	12	13	14	15	16	17
18	19	20	21	22	23	24
25	26	27	28	29	30	31

APR ㉘						
SUN	MON	TUE	WED	THU	FRI	SAT
1	2	3	4	5	6	7
8	9	10	11	12	13	14
15	16	17	18	19	20	21
22	23	24	25	26	27	28
29	30					

MAY ㉙						
SUN	MON	TUE	WED	THU	FRI	SAT
		1	2	3	4	5
6	7	8	9	10	11	12
13	14	15	16	17	18	19
20	21	22	23	24	25	26
27	28	29	30	31		

JUN ㉚						
SUN	MON	TUE	WED	THU	FRI	SAT
					1	2
3	4	5	6	7	8	9
10	11	12	13	14	15	16
17	18	19	20	21	22	23
24	25	26	27	28	29	30

JUL ㉛						
SUN	MON	TUE	WED	THU	FRI	SAT
1	2	3	4	5	6	7
8	9	10	11	12	13	14
15	16	17	18	19	20	21
22	23	24	25	26	27	28
29	30	31				

AUG ㉜						
SUN	MON	TUE	WED	THU	FRI	SAT
			1	2	3	4
5	6	7	8	9	10	11
12	13	14	15	16	17	18
19	20	21	22	23	24	25
26	27	28	29	30	31	

SEP ㉝						
SUN	MON	TUE	WED	THU	FRI	SAT
						1
2	3	4	5	6	7	8
9	10	11	12	13	14	15
16	17	18	19	20	21	22
23/30	24	25	26	27	28	29

OCT ㉞						
SUN	MON	TUE	WED	THU	FRI	SAT
	1	2	3	4	5	6
7	8	9	10	11	12	13
14	15	16	17	18	19	20
21	22	23	24	25	26	27
28	29	30	31			

NOV ㉟						
SUN	MON	TUE	WED	THU	FRI	SAT
				1	2	3
4	5	6	7	8	9	10
11	12	13	14	15	16	17
18	19	20	21	22	23	24
25	26	27	28	29	30	

DEC ㊱						
SUN	MON	TUE	WED	THU	FRI	SAT
						1
2	3	4	5	6	7	8
9	10	11	12	13	14	15
16	17	18	19	20	21	22
23/30	24/31	25	26	27	28	29

MARCH 21 ㊲
JUNE 21 ㊳
SEPT. 21 ㊴
DEC. 21 ㊵

JUNE 5 — TIM! ㊶
MARCH 2 — ANNIVERSARY ㊷
JULY 4 — INDEPENDENCE DAY — STATE BANK — CLOSED–JULY 4 ㊸
APRIL 4 — EASTER SUNDAY ㊹
MAY 17 — DOCTOR 4:30 ㊺
AUGUST ㊻

Months of the year
Meses do ano
25. January
    janeiro
26. February
    fevereiro
27. March
    março
28. April
    abril
29. May
    maio
30. June
    junho
31. July
    julho
32. August
    agosto
33. September
    setembro
34. October
    outubro
35. November
    novembro
36. December
    dezembro

Seasons
Estações do ano
37. spring
    a primavera
38. summer
    o verão
39. fall
    o outono
40. winter
    o inverno

41. birthday
    o aniversário
42. anniversary
    as bodas
43. legal holiday
    o feriado oficial
44. religious holiday
    o feriado religioso
45. appointment
    a hora marcada
46. vacation
    as férias

Use the new language.
Look at the **ordinal numbers** on page **14.**
Use ordinal numbers to say the date.
It's June 5th. It's the fifth.

Talk about your birthday.
My birthday is in the winter.
My birthday is in January.
My birthday is on January twenty-sixth.

Money Dinheiro

Coins Moedas

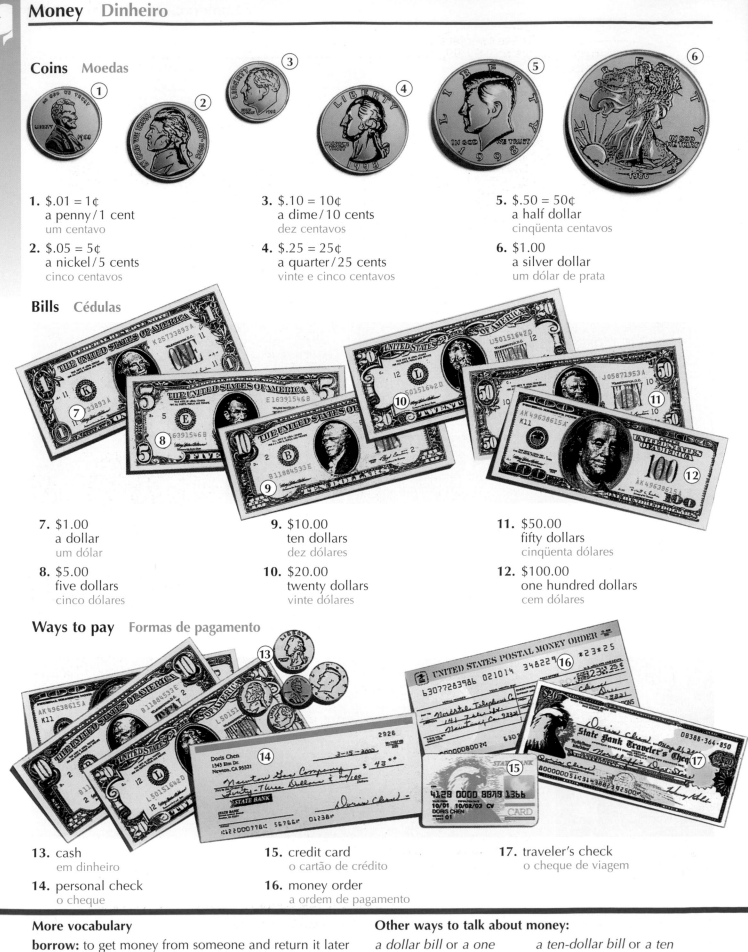

1. $.01 = 1¢
a penny / 1 cent
um centavo

2. $.05 = 5¢
a nickel / 5 cents
cinco centavos

3. $.10 = 10¢
a dime / 10 cents
dez centavos

4. $.25 = 25¢
a quarter / 25 cents
vinte e cinco centavos

5. $.50 = 50¢
a half dollar
cinqüenta centavos

6. $1.00
a silver dollar
um dólar de prata

Bills Cédulas

7. $1.00
a dollar
um dólar

8. $5.00
five dollars
cinco dólares

9. $10.00
ten dollars
dez dólares

10. $20.00
twenty dollars
vinte dólares

11. $50.00
fifty dollars
cinqüenta dólares

12. $100.00
one hundred dollars
cem dólares

Ways to pay Formas de pagamento

13. cash
em dinheiro

14. personal check
o cheque

15. credit card
o cartão de crédito

16. money order
a ordem de pagamento

17. traveler's check
o cheque de viagem

More vocabulary

borrow: to get money from someone and return it later

lend: to give money to someone and get it back later

pay back: to return the money that you borrowed

Other ways to talk about money:

a dollar bill or *a one*

a five-dollar bill or *a five*

a ten-dollar bill or *a ten*

a twenty-dollar bill or *a twenty*

A. **shop** for
comprar

B. **sell**
vender

C. **pay** for/**buy**
pagar / comprar

D. **give**
dar

E. **keep**
guardar

F. **return**
devolver

G. **exchange**
trocar

1. price tag
a etiqueta de preço

2. regular price
o preço normal

3. sale price
o preço de oferta

4. bar code
o código de barras

5. receipt
o cupom fiscal

6. price/cost
o preço / o custo

7. sales tax
o imposto sobre vendas

8. total
o total

9. change
o troco

More vocabulary

When you use a credit card to shop, you get a **bill** in the mail. Bills list, in writing, the items you bought and the total you have to pay.

Share your answers.

1. Name three things you pay for every month.

2. Name one thing you will buy this week.

3. Where do you like to shop?

Age and Physical Description   Idade e descrição física

1. **children**
   as crianças

2. **baby**
   o bebê

3. **toddler**
   a criança pequena

4. **6-year-old boy**
   o menino de 6 anos

5. **10-year-old girl**
   a menina de 10 anos

6. **teenagers**
   os adolescentes

7. **13-year-old boy**
   o menino de 13 anos

8. **19-year-old girl**
   a moça de 19 anos

9. **adults**
   os adultos

10. **woman**
    a mulher

11. **man**
    o homem

12. **senior citizen**
    a pessoa da
    terceira-idade

13. **young**
    o jovem

14. **middle-aged**
    de meia-idade

15. **elderly**
    idoso(a)

16. **tall**
    alto(a)

17. **average height**
    de estatura média

18. **short**
    baixo(a)

19. **pregnant**
    grávida

20. **heavyset**
    troncudo / corpulento

21. **average weight**
    de peso médio

22. **thin/slim**
    magro(a) / esbelto(a)

23. **attractive**
    atraente

24. **cute**
    gracioso(a)

25. **physically challenged**
    deficiente físico

26. **sight impaired/blind**
    deficiente visual / cego(a)

27. **hearing impaired/deaf**
    deficiente auditivo /
    surdo(a)

Talk about yourself and your teacher.

I am _young_, _average height_, and _average weight_.
My teacher is _a middle-aged_, _tall_, _thin_ man.

Use the new language.
Turn to **Hobbies and Games,** pages **162–163.**
Describe each person on the page.
He's _a heavy-set_, _short_, _senior citizen_.

1. short hair o cabelo curto	**7.** sideburns as costeletas	**14.** red hair o cabelo ruivo	**21.** rollers os bobes
2. shoulder-length hair o cabelo na altura do ombro	**8.** bangs a franja	**15.** black hair o cabelo preto	**22.** comb o pente
3. long hair o cabelo comprido	**9.** straight hair o cabelo liso	**16.** blond hair o cabelo loiro	**A.** **cut** hair **cortar** o cabelo
4. part a risca	**10.** wavy hair o cabelo ondulado	**17.** brown hair o cabelo castanho	**B.** **perm** hair **fazer permanente**
5. mustache o bigode	**11.** curly hair o cabelo encaracolado	**18.** brush a escova	**C.** **set** hair **fazer penteado**
6. beard a barba	**12.** bald a careca	**19.** scissors a tesoura	**D.** **color** hair / **dye** hair **tingir** o cabelo
	13. gray hair o cabelo grisalho / branco	**20.** blow dryer o secador de cabelo	

More vocabulary

hair stylist: a person who cuts, sets, and perms hair

hair salon: the place where a hair stylist works

Talk about your hair.

My hair is <u>long</u>, <u>straight</u>, and <u>brown</u>.

I have <u>long</u>, <u>straight</u>, <u>brown</u> hair.

When I was a child my hair was <u>short</u>, <u>curly</u>, and <u>blond</u>.

Tom Lee's Family

1. grandparents
os avós

Min

Lu

2. grandmother
a avó

3. grandfather
o avô

4. parents
os pais

Rose

Chang

Helen

Daniel

5. mother
a mãe

6. father
o pai

10. aunt
a tia

11. uncle
o tio

Tom

Lily

Alex

Emily

8. sister
a irmã

9. brother
o irmão

12. cousin
a prima

7. (Min and Lu's)
grandson
o neto
(de Min e Lu)

Berta

Mario

Ana Garcia's
Family

Ana

13. mother-in-law
a sogra

14. father-in-law
o sogro

Marta

Carlos

Tito

20. (Tito's) wife
a mulher /
a esposa (de Tito)

15. sister-in-law
a cunhada

16. brother-in-law
o cunhado

19. husband
o marido / o esposo

Alice

Eddie

Sara

Felix

17. niece
a sobrinha

18. nephew
o sobrinho

21. daughter
a filha

22. son
o filho

More vocabulary

Lily and Emily are Min and Lu's **granddaughters.**

Daniel is Min and Lu's **son-in-law.**

Ana is Berta and Mario's **daughter-in-law.**

Share your answers.

1. How many brothers and sisters do you have?

2. What number son or daughter are you?

3. Do you have any children?

Lisa Smith's Family

23. married
casados

24. divorced
divorciados

Carol *Dan*

Lisa

25. single mother
a mãe solteira

26. single father
o pai solteiro

27. remarried
casados
novamente

Rick *Carol*

Dan *Sue*

Rick *Carol*

Lisa

Dan *Sue*

28. stepfather
o padrasto

31. stepmother
a madrasta

David *Mary*

Kim *Bill*

29. half brother
o meio-irmão
(irmão por parte
de mãe ou pai)

30. half sister
a meia-irmã (irmã
por parte de mãe
ou pai)

32. stepsister
a meia-irmã
(enteada da
mãe ou do pai)

33. stepbrother
o meio-irmão
(enteado da
mãe ou do pai)

More vocabulary

Carol is Dan's **former wife**.

Sue is Dan's **wife**.

Dan is Carol's **former husband**.

Rick is Carol's **husband**.

Lisa is the **stepdaughter** of both Rick and Sue.

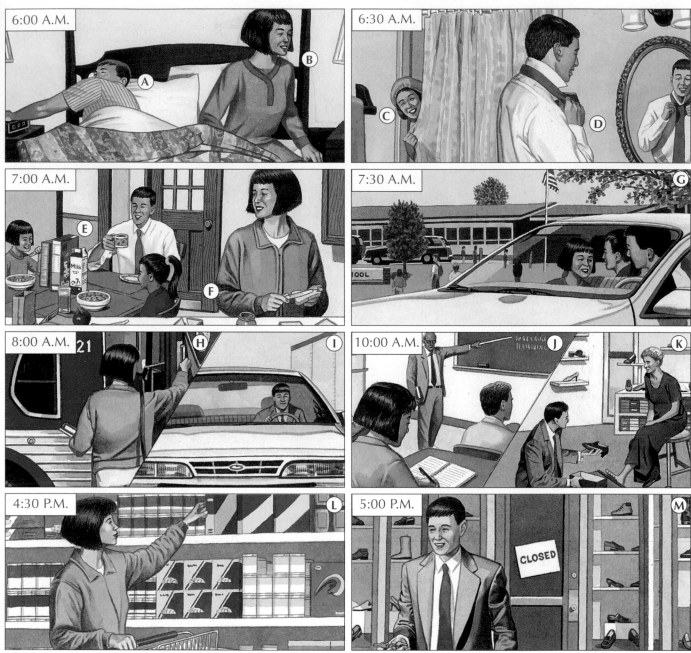

A. **wake up**
acordar

B. **get up**
levantar-se

C. **take** a shower
tomar um banho (de chuveiro)

D. **get dressed**
vestir-se

E. **eat** breakfast
tomar café da manhã

F. **make** lunch
preparar o almoço

G. **take** the children to school
levar os filhos para a escola

H. **take** the bus to school
tomar o ônibus para a escola

I. **drive** to work / **go** to work
ir de carro para o trabalho / ir para o trabalho

J. **be** in school
estar na escola / estudar

K. **work**
trabalhar

L. **go** to the market
ir ao mercado

M. **leave** work
sair do trabalho

Grammar point: 3rd person singular
For **he** and **she**, we add **-s** or **-es** to the verb.
He/She wakes up.
He/She watches TV.

These verbs are different (irregular):
be   *He/She **is** in school at 10:00 a.m.*
have   *He/She **has** dinner at 6:30 p.m.*

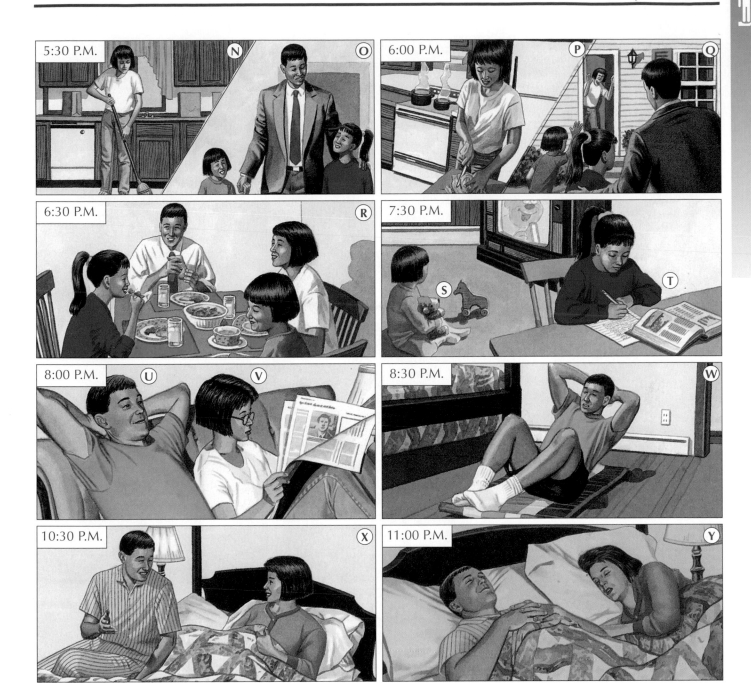

N. clean the house
limpar a casa

O. pick up the children
pegar as crianças

P. cook dinner
fazer o jantar

Q. come home/**get** home
vir para casa / **chegar** em casa

R. have dinner
jantar

S. watch TV
assistir televisão

T. do homework
fazer lição de casa

U. relax
descansar

V. read the paper
ler o jornal

W. exercise
fazer exercícios

X. go to bed
deitar-se

Y. go to sleep
dormir

Talk about your daily routine.

I take _a shower_ in _the morning_.

I go to _school_ in _the evening_.

I go to _bed_ at _11 o'clock_.

Share your answers.

1. Who makes dinner in your family?

2. Who goes to the market?

3. Who goes to work?

A. be born
nascer

B. start school
entrar na escola

C. immigrate
imigrar

D. graduate
formar-se

E. learn to drive
aprender a dirigir

F. join the army
entrar no exército

G. get a job
arrumar um emprego

H. become a citizen
tornar-se um cidadão

I. rent an apartment
alugar um apartamento

J. go to college
entrar na faculdade / na
universidade

K. fall in love
apaixonar-se

L. get married
casar-se

Grammar point: past tense

start		immigrate		be	— was	have	— had
learn		graduate		get	— got	buy	— bought
join	+ed	move	+d	become	— became		
rent		retire		go	— went		
travel		die		fall	— fell		

These verbs are different (irregular):

M. have a baby
ter um bebê

N. travel
viajar

O. buy a house
comprar uma casa

P. move
mudar-se

Q. have a grandchild
ter um neto

R. die
morrer

1. birth certificate
a certidão de nascimento

2. diploma
o diploma

3. Resident Alien card
o cartão de residente permanente

4. driver's license
a carteira de motorista

5. Social Security card
o cartão de previdência social

6. Certificate of Naturalization
a certidão de naturalização

7. college degree
o diploma da faculdade

8. marriage license
a certidão de casamento

9. passport
o passaporte

More vocabulary

When a husband dies, his wife becomes a **widow**.
When a wife dies, her husband becomes a **widower**.
When older people stop working, we say they **retire**.

Talk about yourself.

I was born in 1968.
I learned to drive in 1987.
I immigrated in 1990.

Feelings   Estados de espírito e sensações

1. hot
   estar com calor
2. thirsty
   estar com sede
3. sleepy
   estar com sono

4. cold
   estar com frio
5. hungry
   estar com fome
6. full
   estar satisfeito

7. comfortable
   confortável
8. uncomfortable
   desconfortável
9. disgusted
   enojado(a)
10. calm
    tranqüilo(a)
11. nervous
    nervoso(a) / aflito(a)

12. in pain
    com dor
13. worried
    preocupado(a)
14. sick
    doente
15. well
    bem
16. relieved
    aliviado(a)

17. hurt
    magoado(a)
18. lonely
    solitário(a)
19. in love
    apaixonado(a)

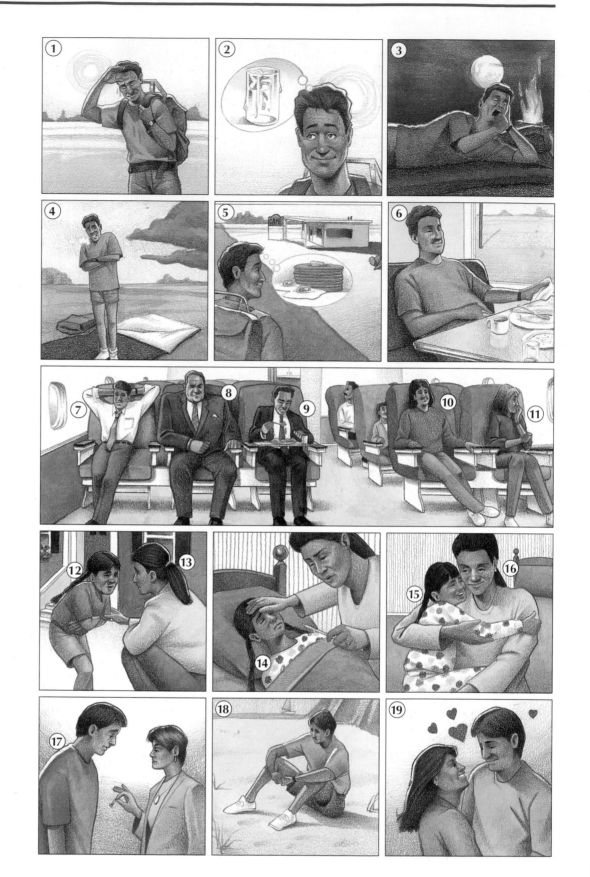

More vocabulary

furious: very angry

terrified: very scared

overjoyed: very happy

exhausted: very tired

starving: very hungry

humiliated: very embarrassed

Talk about your feelings.

I feel <u>happy</u> when I see <u>my friends</u>.

I feel <u>homesick</u> when I think about <u>my family</u>.

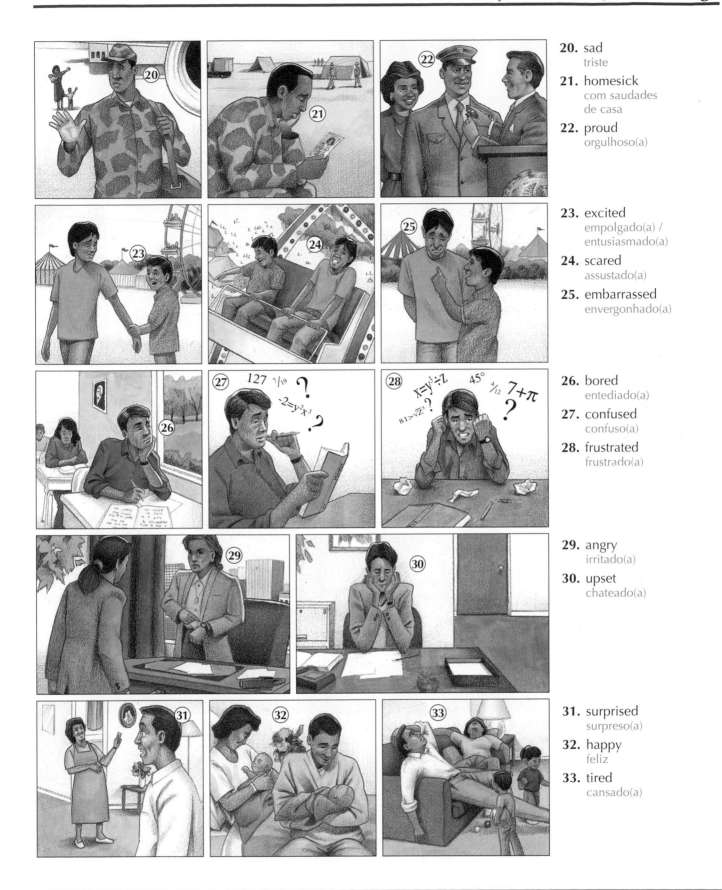

20. sad
    triste
21. homesick
    com saudades
    de casa
22. proud
    orgulhoso(a)

23. excited
    empolgado(a) /
    entusiasmado(a)
24. scared
    assustado(a)
25. embarrassed
    envergonhado(a)

26. bored
    entediado(a)
27. confused
    confuso(a)
28. frustrated
    frustrado(a)

29. angry
    irritado(a)
30. upset
    chateado(a)

31. surprised
    surpreso(a)
32. happy
    feliz
33. tired
    cansado(a)

Use the new language.

Look at **Clothing I,** page **64,** and answer the questions.

1. How does the runner feel?

2. How does the man at the bus stop feel?

3. How does the woman at the bus stop feel?

4. How do the teenagers feel?

5. How does the little boy feel?

A Graduation Uma formatura

The Ceremony

1. **graduating class**
   a classe de formandos

2. **gown**
   a beca

3. **cap**
   o capelo

4. **stage**
   o palco

5. **podium**
   a tribuna

6. **graduate**
   o(a) formando(a)

7. **diploma**
   o diploma

8. **valedictorian**
   a oradora da turma

9. **guest speaker**
   o orador convidado

10. **audience**
    o público

11. **photographer**
    o fotógrafo

A. **graduate**
   formar-se / receber o
   diploma

B. **applaud / clap**
   aplaudir

C. **cry**
   chorar

D. **take** a picture
   tirar uma foto

E. **give** a speech
   fazer um discurso

Talk about what the people in the pictures are doing.

She is [tak**ing** a picture.
          giv**ing** a speech.
          smil**ing**.
          laugh**ing**.

He is [mak**ing** a toast.
          clap**ping**.

They are [graduat**ing**.
             hug**ging**.
             kiss**ing**.
             applaud**ing**.

The Party

12. caterer
    o fornecedor de serviço
    de buffet

13. buffet
    o buffet

14. guests
    os convidados

15. banner
    a faixa

16. dance floor
    a pista de dança

17. DJ (disc jockey)
    o DJ (o disc jockey)

18. gifts
    os presentes

F. kiss
   beijar

G. hug
   abraçar

H. laugh
   rir

I. make a toast
   brindar

J. dance
   dançar

Share your answers.

1. Did you ever go to a graduation? Whose?

2. Did you ever give a speech? Where?

3. Did you ever hear a great speaker? Where?

4. Did you ever go to a graduation party?

5. What do you like to eat at parties?

6. Do you like to dance at parties?

33

Places to Live   Lugares para morar

1. the city / an urban area
a cidade / uma área urbana

2. the suburbs
os subúrbios / os bairros afastados

3. a small town
uma cidade pequena

4. the country / a rural area
o campo / uma área rural

5. apartment building
o prédio de apartamentos

6. house
a casa

7. townhouse
a casa de conjunto residencial

8. mobile home
a casa-trailer

9. college dormitory
a residência universitária

10. shelter
o abrigo

11. nursing home
o asilo

12. ranch
a fazenda de criação
(de cavalos e gado)

13. farm
a fazenda / o sítio

More vocabulary

duplex house: a house divided into two homes

condominium: an apartment building where each apartment is owned separately

co-op: an apartment building owned by the residents

Share your answers.

1. Do you like where you live?
2. Where did you live in your country?
3. What types of housing are there near your school?

Renting an apartment   Alugando um apartamento

A. look for a new apartment
procurar um apartamento novo

B. talk to the manager
conversar com o administrador /
o síndico

C. sign a rental agreement
assinar um contrato de aluguel

D. move in
mudar-se

E. unpack
desempacotar

F. pay the rent
pagar o aluguel

Buying a house   Comprando uma casa

G. talk to the Realtor
falar com o corretor

H. make an offer
fazer uma oferta

I. get a loan
fazer um empréstimo

J. take ownership
pegar as chaves

K. arrange the furniture
arrumar os móveis

L. pay the mortgage
pagar a (prestação da) hipoteca

More vocabulary

lease: a rental agreement for a specific period of time
utilities: gas, water, and electricity for the home

Practice talking to an apartment manager.

How much is the rent?
Are utilities included?
When can I move in?

1. first floor
o térreo

2. second floor
o primeiro andar

3. third floor
o segundo andar

4. fourth floor
o terceiro andar

5. roof garden
o jardim na cobertura

6. playground
o playground

7. fire escape
a escada de emergência / de incêndio

8. intercom / speaker
o interfone

9. security system
o sistema de segurança

10. doorman
o porteiro

11. vacancy sign
a placa de "Aluga-se"

12. manager / superintendent
o administrador / o síndico

13. security gate
o portão de segurança

14. storage locker
o armário para depósito

15. parking space
a vaga na garagem

More vocabulary

rec room: a short way of saying **recreation room**

basement: the area below the street level of an apartment or a house

Talk about where you live.

I live in Apartment 3 near the entrance.

I live in Apartment 11 on the second floor near the fire escape.

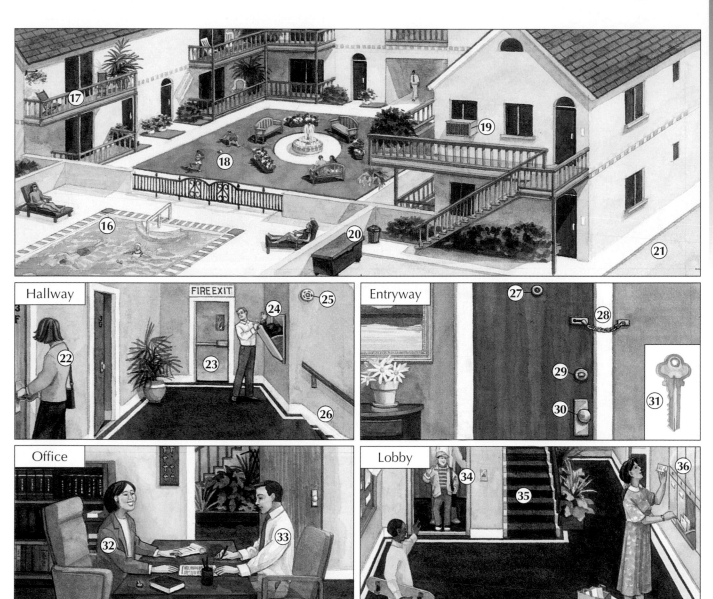

16. swimming pool a piscina	**23.** fire exit a saída de emergência / de incêndio	**30.** doorknob a maçaneta
17. balcony a sacada	**24.** trash chute a lixeira	**31.** key a chave
18. courtyard o pátio	**25.** smoke detector o detector de fumaça	**32.** landlord a proprietária
19. air conditioner o ar-condicionado	**26.** stairway a escadaria	**33.** tenant o inquilino
20. trash bin o depósito de lixo	**27.** peephole o olho mágico	**34.** elevator o elevador
21. alley a passagem	**28.** door chain o ferrolho	**35.** stairs a escada
22. neighbor o vizinho	**29.** dead-bolt lock a trava de segurança	**36.** mailboxes as caixas de correio

Grammar point: *there is, there are*

singular: *there is*   plural: *there are*

There is a fire exit in the hallway.

There are mailboxes in the lobby.

Talk about apartments.

My apartment has <u>an elevator</u>, <u>a lobby</u>, and <u>a rec room</u>.

My apartment doesn't have <u>a pool</u> or <u>a garage</u>.

My apartment needs <u>air conditioning</u>.

1. **floor plan**
   a planta

2. **backyard**
   o quintal

3. **fence**
   a cerca

4. **mailbox**
   a caixa de correio

5. **driveway**
   a entrada da garagem

6. **garage**
   a garagem

7. **garage door**
   a porta da garagem

8. **screen door**
   a porta de tela

9. **porch light**
   a luz da entrada

10. **doorbell**
    a campainha

11. **front door**
    a porta da frente

12. **storm door**
    a contra-porta de inverno

13. **steps**
    os degraus

14. **front walk**
    o caminho de entrada

15. **front yard**
    o jardim

16. **deck**
    o terraço

17. **window**
    a janela

18. **shutter**
    a veneziana

19. **gutter**
    a calha

20. **roof**
    o telhado

21. **chimney**
    a chaminé

22. **TV antenna**
    a antena de TV

More vocabulary

two-story house: a house with two floors

downstairs: the bottom floor

upstairs: the part of a house above the bottom floor

Share your answers.

1. What do you like about this house?

2. What's something you don't like about the house?

3. Describe the perfect house.

1. hedge
   a cerca-viva / a sebe

2. hammock
   a rede

3. garbage can
   a lata de lixo

4. leaf blower
   o soprador de folhas

5. patio furniture
   os móveis de jardim

6. patio
   o pátio/o terraço

7. barbecue grill
   a churrasqueira

8. sprinkler
   o irrigador

9. hose
   a mangueira

10. compost pile
    o adubo

11. rake
    o ancinho

12. hedge clippers
    a tesoura grande de
    podar / o tesourão

13. shovel
    a pá

14. trowel
    a colher de transplante

15. pruning shears
    a tesoura pequena
    de podar

16. wheelbarrow
    o carrinho-de-mão

17. watering can
    o regador

18. flowerpot
    o vaso de flores

19. flower
    a flor

20. bush
    o arbusto / a roseira

21. lawn
    o gramado

22. lawn mower
    o cortador de grama

A. **weed** the flower bed
   tirar as ervas daninhas
   do canteiro

B. **water** the plants
   regar as plantas

C. **mow** the lawn
   cortar a grama

D. **plant** a tree
   plantar uma árvore

E. **trim** the hedge
   podar a sebe

F. **rake** the leaves
   ajuntar as folhas

Talk about your yard and gardening.

I like to <u>plant trees</u>.

I don't like to <u>weed</u>.

I like/don't like to work in the yard/garden.

Share your answers.

1. What flowers, trees, or plants do you see in the picture? (Look at **Trees, Plants, and Flowers,** pages **128–129** for help.)

2. Do you ever use a barbecue grill to cook?

1. **cabinet**
   o armário de cozinha

2. **paper towels**
   a toalha de papel

3. **dish drainer**
   o escorredor de louça

4. **dishwasher**
   a lavadora de louça

5. **garbage disposal**
   o triturador de lixo

6. **sink**
   a pia

7. **toaster**
   a torradeira

8. **shelf**
   a prateleira

9. **refrigerator**
   a geladeira

10. **freezer**
    o congelador / o freezer

11. **coffeemaker**
    a cafeteira

12. **blender**
    o liqüidificador

13. **microwave oven**
    o forno de microondas

14. **electric can opener**
    o abridor de lata elétrico

15. **toaster oven**
    o forno elétrico

16. **pot**
    a panela / a caçarola

17. **teakettle**
    a chaleira

18. **stove**
    o fogão

19. **burner**
    a boca do fogão

20. **oven**
    o forno

21. **broiler**
    a estufa

22. **counter**
    a balcão

23. **drawer**
    a gaveta

24. **pan**
    a frigideira

25. **electric mixer**
    a batedeira elétrica

26. **food processor**
    o processador de
    alimentos

27. **cutting board**
    a tábua de cortar

Talk about the location of kitchen items.

The toaster oven is on the counter near the stove.

The microwave is above the stove.

Share your answers.

1. Do you have a garbage disposal? a dishwasher? a microwave?

2. Do you eat in the kitchen?

1. **china cabinet**
   a cristaleira

2. **set of dishes**
   o jogo de pratos

3. **platter**
   o prato para servir /
   a travessa

4. **ceiling fan**
   o ventilador de teto

5. **light fixture**
   o lustre

6. **serving dish**
   a travessa

7. **candle**
   a vela

8. **candlestick**
   o castiçal

9. **vase**
   o vaso

10. **tray**
    a bandeja

11. **teapot**
    o bule de chá

12. **sugar bowl**
    o açucareiro

13. **creamer**
    a leiteira

14. **saltshaker**
    o saleiro

15. **pepper shaker**
    o pimenteiro

16. **dining room chair**
    a cadeira da sala
    de jantar

17. **dining room table**
    a mesa de jantar

18. **tablecloth**
    a toalha de mesa

19. **napkin**
    o guardanapo

20. **place mat**
    a toalha de jogo
    americano

21. **fork**
    o garfo

22. **knife**
    a faca

23. **spoon**
    a colher

24. **plate**
    o prato

25. **bowl**
    a tigela

26. **glass**
    o copo

27. **coffee cup**
    a xícara de café

28. **mug**
    a caneca

Practice asking for things in the dining room.

Please pass <u>the platter</u>.

May I have <u>the creamer</u>?

Could I have <u>a fork</u>, please?

Share your answers.

1. What are the women in the picture saying?

2. In your home, where do you eat?

3. Do you like to make dinner for your friends?

41

1. **bookcase**
   a estante de livros

2. **basket**
   a cesta

3. **track lighting**
   a luminária de trilho

4. **lightbulb**
   a lâmpada

5. **ceiling**
   o teto / o forro

6. **wall**
   a parede

7. **painting**
   a pintura

8. **mantel**
   o console da lareira

9. **fireplace**
   a lareira

10. **fire**
    o fogo

11. **fire screen**
    a tela de proteção
    da lareira

12. **logs**
    a lenha

13. **wall unit**
    a estante

14. **stereo system**
    o aparelho de som

15. **floor lamp**
    o abajur de pé

16. **drapes**
    as cortinas

17. **window**
    a janela

18. **plant**
    a planta

19. **sofa / couch**
    o sofá

20. **throw pillow**
    a almofada

21. **end table**
    a mesa de canto

22. **magazine holder**
    o porta-revistas

23. **coffee table**
    a mesa de centro

24. **armchair / easy chair**
    a poltrona

25. **love seat**
    o sofá de dois lugares

26. **TV (television)**
    a TV (o televisor)

27. **carpet**
    o carpete

Use the new language.

Look at **Colors**, page **12**, and describe this room.

There is <u>a gray sofa</u> and <u>a gray armchair</u>.

Talk about your living room.

In my living room I have <u>a sofa</u>, <u>two chairs</u>, and <u>a coffee table</u>.

I don't have <u>a fireplace</u> or <u>a wall unit</u>.

1. **hamper**
   o cesto de roupa suja

2. **bathtub**
   a banheira

3. **rubber mat**
   o tapete de borracha

4. **drain**
   o ralo

5. **hot water**
   a água quente

6. **faucet**
   a torneira

7. **cold water**
   a água fria

8. **towel rack**
   o porta-toalhas

9. **tile**
   o azulejo

10. **showerhead**
    o chuveiro

11. **(mini)blinds**
    a mini-persiana

12. **bath towel**
    a toalha de banho

13. **hand towel**
    a toalha de rosto

14. **washcloth**
    o esfregão de banho

15. **toilet paper**
    o papel higiênico

16. **toilet brush**
    a escova de
    vaso sanitário

17. **toilet**
    o vaso sanitário

18. **mirror**
    o espelho

19. **medicine cabinet**
    o armário de banheiro

20. **toothbrush**
    a escova de dente

21. **toothbrush holder**
    o porta-escova-de-dente

22. **sink**
    a pia

23. **soap**
    o sabonete

24. **soap dish**
    a saboneteira

25. **wastebasket**
    o cestinho de banheiro

26. **scale**
    a balança

27. **bath mat**
    o tapete /
    o piso de banheiro

More vocabulary

half bath: a bathroom without a shower or bathtub

linen closet: a closet or cabinet for towels and sheets

stall shower: a shower without a bathtub

Share your answers.

1. Do you turn off the water when you brush your teeth? wash your hair? shave?

2. Does your bathroom have a bathtub or a stall shower?

1. mirror o espelho	**8.** bed a cama	**15.** headboard a cabeceira	**22.** dust ruffle o babado da cama
2. dresser / bureau a cômoda	**9.** pillow o travesseiro	**16.** clock radio o rádio-relógio	**23.** rug o tapete
3. drawer a gaveta	**10.** pillowcase a fronha	**17.** lamp o abajur	**24.** floor o piso
4. closet o armário / o guarda-roupa	**11.** bedspread a colcha	**18.** lampshade a cúpula do abajur	**25.** mattress o colchão
5. curtains as cortinas	**12.** blanket o cobertor	**19.** light switch o interruptor de luz	**26.** box spring a cama box
6. window shade a persiana	**13.** flat sheet o lençol de cima	**20.** outlet a tomada	**27.** bed frame a armação da cama / a "frame"
7. photograph a fotografia	**14.** fitted sheet o lençol de baixo.	**21.** night table o criado-mudo	

Use the new language.

Describe this room. (See **Describing Things,** page **11,** for help.)

I see <u>a soft pillow</u> and <u>a beautiful bedspread</u>.

Share your answers.

1. What is your favorite thing in your bedroom?

2. Do you have a clock in your bedroom? Where is it?

3. Do you have a mirror in your bedroom? Where is it?

1. bunk bed
   o beliche

2. comforter
   o acolchoado

3. night-light
   a luz sentinela

4. mobile
   o móbile

5. wallpaper
   o papel de parede

6. crib
   o berço

7. bumper pad
   o protetor de berço

8. chest of drawers
   a cômoda

9. baby monitor
   a babá eletrônica

10. teddy bear
    o ursinho

11. smoke detector
    o detector de fumaça

12. changing table
    o trocador

13. diaper pail
    o recipiente para
    fraldas usadas

14. dollhouse
    a casa de bonecas

15. blocks
    os blocos

16. ball
    a bola

17. picture book
    o livro com figuras

18. doll
    a boneca

19. cradle
    o bercinho de boneca

20. coloring book
    o livro para colorir

21. crayons
    os lápis de cera

22. puzzle
    o quebra-cabeça

23. stuffed animals
    os bichinhos de pelúcia

24. toy chest
    o baú de brinquedos

Talk about where items are in the room.

The dollhouse is near _the coloring book_.

The teddy bear is on _the chest of drawers_.

Share your answers.

1. Do you think this is a good room for children? Why?

2. What toys did you play with when you were a child?

3. What children's stories do you know?

A. **dust** the furniture
   tirar o pó dos móveis

B. **recycle** the newspapers
   reciclar jornais

C. **clean** the oven
   limpar o forno

D. **wash** the windows
   limpar os vidros

E. **sweep** the floor
   varrer o chão

F. **empty** the wastebasket
   esvaziar o lixo

G. **make** the bed
   arrumar a cama

H. **put away** the toys
   guardar os brinquedos

I. **vacuum** the carpet
   passar o aspirador de pó no carpete

J. **mop** the floor
   limpar o chão **com esfregão**

K. **polish** the furniture
   lustrar os móveis

L. **scrub** the floor
   esfregar o chão

M. **wash** the dishes
   lavar a louça

N. **dry** the dishes
   enxugar a louça

O. **wipe** the counter
   limpar o balcão

P. **change** the sheets
   trocar a roupa de cama

Q. **take out** the garbage
   levar o lixo para fora

Talk about yourself.

I wash __the dishes__ every day.
I change __the sheets__ every week.
I never __dry the dishes__.

Share your answers.

1. Who does the housework in your family?
2. What is your favorite cleaning job?
3. What is your least favorite cleaning job?

1. feather duster
o espanador

2. recycling bin
o recipiente para reciclagem

3. oven cleaner
o limpador de forno

4. rubber gloves
as luvas de borracha

5. steel-wool soap pads
a esponja de aço com sabão

6. rags
os panos de limpeza

7. stepladder
a escadinha

8. glass cleaner
o limpador de vidros / limpa-vidros

9. squeegee
o rodinho para vidro

10. broom
a vassoura

11. dustpan
a pá de lixo

12. trash bags
os sacos de lixo

13. vacuum cleaner
o aspirador de pó

14. vacuum cleaner attachments
os acessórios do aspirador de pó

15. vacuum cleaner bag
o saco para aspirador de pó

16. wet mop
o esfregão (para limpar piso)

17. dust mop
o esfregão (para polir / varrer assoalho)

18. furniture polish
o lustra-móveis

19. scrub brush
a escova para esfregar

20. bucket / pail
o balde

21. dishwashing liquid
o detergente

22. dish towel
o pano de prato

23. cleanser
o limpador

24. sponge
a esponja

Practice asking for the items.

I want to <u>wash the windows</u>.
Please hand me <u>the squeegee</u>.

I have to <u>sweep the floor</u>.
Can you get me <u>the broom</u>, please?

Household Problems and Repairs   Problemas domésticos e consertos

1. The water heater is **not working**.
   O aquecedor de água **não** está **funcionando**.

2. The power is **out**.
   Acabou a força. / Está faltando força.

3. The roof is **leaking**.
   O telhado tem **goteiras**.

4. The wall is **cracked**.
   A parede está **com rachaduras**.

5. The window is **broken**.
   O vidro está **quebrado**.

6. The lock is **broken**.
   A fechadura está **quebrada**.

7. The steps are **broken**.
   Os degraus estão **quebrados**.

8. roofer
   o profissional que conserta telhados

9. electrician
   o eletricista

10. repair person
    o profissional que faz consertos gerais

11. locksmith
    o chaveiro

12. carpenter
    o carpinteiro

13. fuse box
    a caixa de fusíveis

14. gas meter
    o medidor de gás

Use the new language.
Look at **Tools and Building Supplies,** pages **150–151.**
Name the tools you use for household repairs.

I use a hammer and nails to fix a broken step.
I use a wrench to repair a dripping faucet.

15. The furnace is **broken**.
O sistema de aquecimento está **quebrado**.

16. The faucet is **dripping**.
A torneira está **pingando**.

17. The sink is **overflowing**.
A pia está **transbordando**.

18. The toilet is **stopped up**.
O vaso sanitário está **entupido**.

19. The pipes are **frozen**.
A tubulação está **congelada**.

20. plumber
o encanador

21. exterminator
o dedetizador

Household pests
Pragas domésticas

22. termite(s)
o(s) cupim(ns)

23. flea(s)
a(s) pulga(s)

24. ant(s)
a(s) formiga(s)

25. cockroach(es)
a(s) barata(s)

26. mice*
os camundongos

27. rat(s)
o(s) rato(s)

*Note: *one mouse, two mice*

More vocabulary

fix: to repair something that is broken

exterminate: to kill household pests

pesticide: a chemical that is used to kill household pests

Share your answers.

1. Who does household repairs in your home?

2. What is the worst problem a home can have?

3. What is the most expensive problem a home can have?

49

Fruit   Frutas

TODAY
BANANAS 2lb/1.00
BLUEBERRIES 1.99 pint

1. grapes as uvas	**9. grapefruit** as toranjas / toronjas	**17. strawberries** os morangos	**24. watermelons** as melancias
2. pineapples os abacaxis	**10. oranges** as laranjas	**18. raspberries** as framboesas	**25. dates** as tâmaras
3. bananas as bananas	**11. lemons** os limões (amarelos)	**19. blueberries** os blueberry / fruto do mirtilo	**26. prunes** as ameixas secas
4. apples as maçãs	**12. limes** os limões (verdes)	**20. papayas** os mamões	**27. raisins** as uvas-passas
5. peaches os pêssegos	**13. tangerines** as tangerinas	**21. mangoes** as mangas	**28. not ripe** verde
6. pears as pêras	**14. avocadoes** os abacates	**22. coconuts** os cocos	**29. ripe** maduro(a)
7. apricots os damascos	**15. cantaloupes** os melões	**23. nuts** as castanhas	**30. rotten** podre / passado(a)
8. plums as ameixas	**16. cherries** as cerejas		

Language note: *a bunch of*

We say *a bunch of grapes* and *a bunch of bananas.*

Share your answers.

1. Which fruits do you put in a fruit salad?
2. Which fruits are sold in your area in the summer?
3. What fruits did you have in your country?

1. lettuce
   a alface

2. cabbage
   o repolho

3. carrots
   as cenouras

4. zucchini
   a abobrinha

5. radishes
   os rabanetes

6. beets
   as beterrabas

7. sweet peppers
   os pimentões

8. chili peppers
   as pimentas

9. celery
   o aipo

10. parsley
    a salsinha

11. spinach
    o espinafre

12. cucumbers
    os pepinos

13. squash
    a abóbora

14. turnips
    os nabos

15. broccoli
    o brócolis

16. cauliflower
    a couve-flor

17. scallions
    a cebolinha verde

18. eggplants
    as berinjelas

19. peas
    as ervilhas

20. artichokes
    os alcachofras

21. potatoes
    as batatas

22. yams
    as batatas-doces

23. tomatoes
    os tomates

24. asparagus
    os aspargos

25. string beans
    as vagens

26. mushrooms
    os cogumelos

27. corn
    o milho

28. onions
    as cebolas

29. garlic
    o alho

Language note: *a bunch of, a head of*

We say *a bunch of carrots, a bunch of celery,* and *a bunch of spinach.*

We say *a head of lettuce, a head of cabbage,* and *a head of cauliflower.*

Share your answers.

1. Which vegetables do you eat raw? cooked?

2. Which vegetables need to be in the refrigerator?

3. Which vegetables don't need to be in the refrigerator?

Beef   Carne de vaca

1. roast beef
o rosbife / a carne assada

2. steak
o filé / o bife

3. stewing beef
a carne para cozido

4. ground beef
a carne moída

5. beef ribs
as costelas de vaca

6. veal cutlets
as costeletas de vitela

7. liver
o fígado

8. tripe
o bucho

Pork   Carne de porco

9. ham
o presunto

10. pork chops
as bistecas de porco

11. bacon
o bacon / o toucinho

12. sausage
a lingüiça

Lamb   Carne de carneiro

13. lamb shanks
o pernil de carneiro

14. leg of lamb
a perna de carneiro

15. lamb chops
as costeletas de carneiro

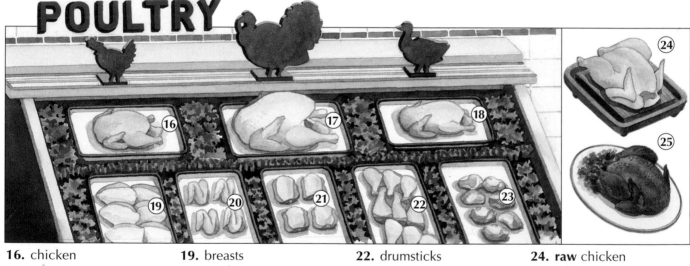

16. chicken
o frango

17. turkey
o peru

18. duck
o pato

19. breasts
o peito

20. wings
as asas

21. thighs
as sobrecoxas

22. drumsticks
as coxas

23. gizzards
as moelas

24. **raw** chicken
o frango **cru**

25. **cooked** chicken
o frango **cozido**

More vocabulary

vegetarian: a person who doesn't eat meat

Meat and poultry without bones are called **boneless**.

Poultry without skin is called **skinless**.

Share your answers.

1. What kind of meat do you eat most often?

2. What kind of meat do you use in soup?

3. What part of the chicken do you like the most?

DELI

1. **white bread**
   o pão de fôrma branco

2. **wheat bread**
   o pão de fôrma de trigo

3. **rye bread**
   o pão de centeio

4. **smoked turkey**
   o peru defumado

5. **salami**
   o salame

6. **pastrami**
   o pastrami (carne defumada)

7. **roast beef**
   o rosbife / a carne assada

8. **corned beef**
   a carne salgada

9. **American cheese**
   o queijo prato

10. **cheddar cheese**
    o queijo cheddar

11. **Swiss cheese**
    o queijo suíço

12. **jack cheese**
    o queijo tipo jack

13. **potato salad**
    a salada de batata

14. **coleslaw**
    a salada de repolho

15. **pasta salad**
    a salada de macarrão

SEAFOOD

Fish Peixe

16. **trout**
    a truta

17. **catfish**
    o bagre

18. **whole salmon**
    o salmão inteiro

19. **salmon steak**
    a posta de salmão

20. **halibut**
    o linguado gigante

21. **filet of sole**
    o filé de linguado

Shellfish Moluscos e crustáceos

22. **crab**
    o caranguejo

23. **lobster**
    a lagosta

24. **shrimp**
    o camarão

25. **scallops**
    as vieiras

26. **mussels**
    os mexilhões

27. **oysters**
    as ostras

28. **clams**
    os mariscos / as almêijoas

29. **fresh** fish
    o peixe **fresco**

30. **frozen** fish
    o peixe **congelado**

Practice ordering a sandwich.

I'd like roast beef and American cheese on rye bread.

Tell what you want on it.

Please put tomato, lettuce, onions, and mustard on it.

Share your answers.

1. Do you like to eat fish?
2. Do you buy fresh or frozen fish?

1. **bottle return**
   a devolução de garrafas
2. **meat and poultry section**
   a seção de carnes e aves
3. **shopping cart**
   o carrinho de compras
4. **canned goods**
   os produtos enlatados
5. **aisle**
   o corredor
6. **baked goods**
   os produtos de panificadora
7. **shopping basket**
   o cesta de compras
8. **manager**
   a gerente
9. **dairy section**
   a seção de laticínios
10. **pet food**
    a comida para animais
11. **produce section**
    a seção de frutas e verduras

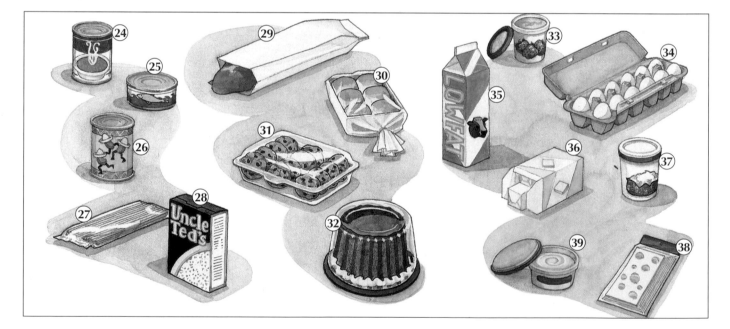

24. **soup**
    a sopa
25. **tuna**
    o atum
26. **beans**
    o feijão
27. **spaghetti**
    o espaguete
28. **rice**
    o arroz
29. **bread**
    o pão
30. **rolls**
    os pãezinhos
31. **cookies**
    os biscoitos
32. **cake**
    o bolo
33. **yogurt**
    o iogurte
34. **eggs**
    os ovos
35. **milk**
    o leite
36. **butter**
    a manteiga
37. **sour cream**
    o creme de leite azedo
38. **cheese**
    o queijo
39. **margarine**
    a margarina

12. frozen foods
as comidas congeladas

13. baking products
os produtos para
pães e bolos

14. paper products
os produtos de papel

15. beverages
as bebidas

16. snack foods
as guloseimas

17. checkstand
o (balcão do) caixa

18. cash register
a caixa registradora

19. checker
a caixa

20. line
a fila

21. bagger
a empacotadora

22. paper bag
o saco de papel

23. plastic bag
a sacola de plástico

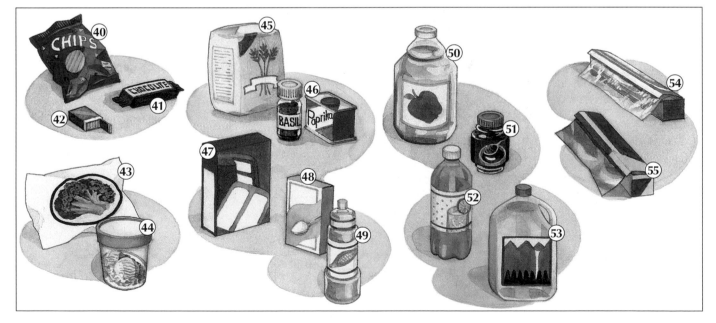

40. potato chips
a batata frita

41. candy bar
o chocolate

42. gum
o chiclete

43. frozen vegetables
as verduras e legumes
congelados

44. ice cream
o sorvete

45. flour
a farinha

46. spices
os temperos

47. cake mix
a mistura para bolo

48. sugar
o açúcar

49. oil
o óleo

50. apple juice
o suco de maçã

51. instant coffee
o café solúvel

52. soda
o refrigerante

53. bottled water
a garrafa de água

54. plastic wrap
o filme transparente
de PVC

55. aluminum foil
o papel-alumínio

Containers and Packaged Foods   Recipientes e alimentos embalados

1. bottle
a garrafa

2. jar
o frasco

3. can
a lata

4. carton
a caixa /
a embalagem
longa-vida

5. container
o pote

6. box
a caixa

7. bag
o saco

8. package
o pacote

9. six-pack
a embalagem
com 6

10. loaf
o filão / o pão
de fôrma

11. roll
o rolo

12. tube
o tubo

13. a bottle of soda
uma garrafa de refrigerante

14. a jar of jam
um vidro de geléia

15. a can of soup
uma lata de sopa

16. a carton of eggs
uma caixa de ovos

17. a container of cottage cheese
um pote de queijo tipo cottage

18. a box of cereal
uma caixa de cereal

19. a bag of flour
um saco / pacote de farinha

20. a package of cookies
um pacote de biscoito

21. a six-pack of soda
uma embalagem de 6 refrigerantes

22. a loaf of bread
um pão de fôrma

23. a roll of paper towels
um rolo de toalha de papel

24. a tube of toothpaste
um tubo de pasta de dente

Grammar point: *How much? How many?*

Some foods can be counted: *one apple, two apples.*

How many apples do you need? I need **two** apples.

Some foods cannot be counted, like liquids, grains, spices, or dairy foods. For these, count containers: *one box of rice, two boxes of rice.*

How much rice do you need? *I need* **two boxes.**

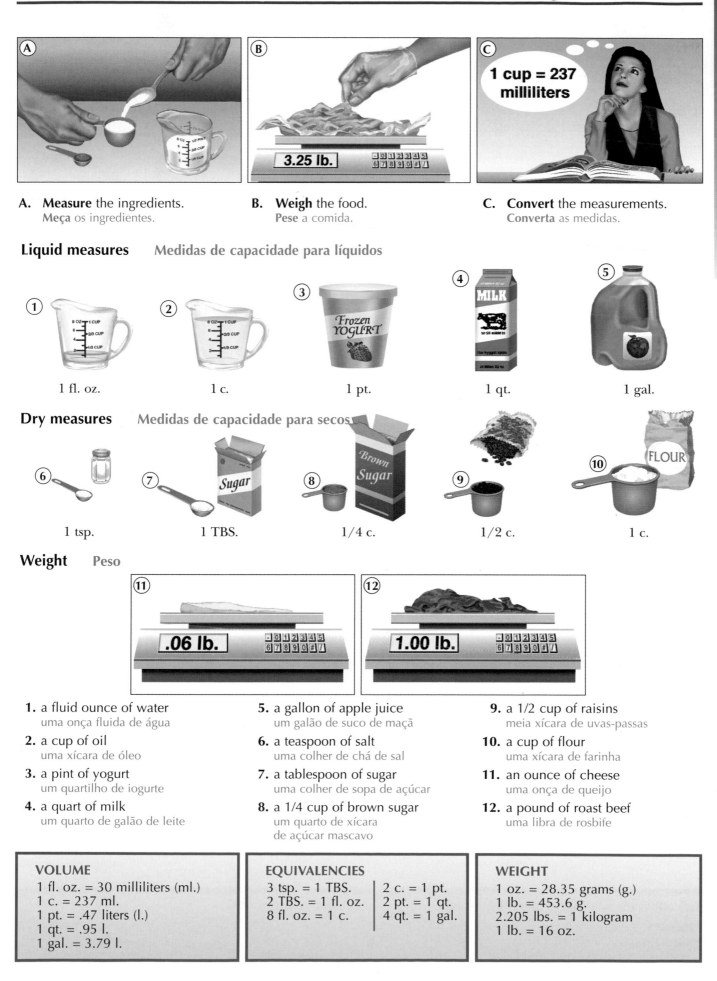

A. Measure the ingredients.
Meça os ingredientes.

B. Weigh the food.
Pese a comida.

C. Convert the measurements.
Converta as medidas.

1 cup = 237 milliliters

Liquid measures   Medidas de capacidade para líquidos

1 fl. oz.   1 c.   1 pt.   1 qt.   1 gal.

Dry measures   Medidas de capacidade para secos

1 tsp.   1 TBS.   1/4 c.   1/2 c.   1 c.

Weight   Peso

.06 lb.   1.00 lb.

1. a fluid ounce of water
uma onça fluida de água

2. a cup of oil
uma xícara de óleo

3. a pint of yogurt
um quartilho de iogurte

4. a quart of milk
um quarto de galão de leite

5. a gallon of apple juice
um galão de suco de maçã

6. a teaspoon of salt
uma colher de chá de sal

7. a tablespoon of sugar
uma colher de sopa de açúcar

8. a 1/4 cup of brown sugar
um quarto de xícara
de açúcar mascavo

9. a 1/2 cup of raisins
meia xícara de uvas-passas

10. a cup of flour
uma xícara de farinha

11. an ounce of cheese
uma onça de queijo

12. a pound of roast beef
uma libra de rosbife

VOLUME
1 fl. oz. = 30 milliliters (ml.)
1 c. = 237 ml.
1 pt. = .47 liters (l.)
1 qt. = .95 l.
1 gal. = 3.79 l.

EQUIVALENCIES
3 tsp. = 1 TBS.   2 c. = 1 pt.
2 TBS. = 1 fl. oz. 2 pt. = 1 qt.
8 fl. oz. = 1 c.   4 qt. = 1 gal.

WEIGHT
1 oz. = 28.35 grams (g.)
1 lb. = 453.6 g.
2.205 lbs. = 1 kilogram
1 lb. = 16 oz.

Food Preparation   Preparo de alimentos

Scrambled eggs   Ovos mexidos

A. **Break** 3 eggs.
   Quebre 3 ovos.
B. **Beat** well.
   Bata bem.
C. **Grease** the pan.
   Unte a frigideira.

D. **Pour** the eggs into the pan.
   Despeje os ovos na frigideira.
E. **Stir.**
   Mexa.
F. **Cook** until done.
   Cozinhe até ficar pronto.

Vegetable casserole   Legumes ao forno

G. **Chop** the onions.
   Pique as cebolas em pedacinhos.
H. **Sauté** the onions.
   Doure as cebolas.
I. **Steam** the broccoli.
   Cozinhe o brócoli no vapor.

J. **Grate** the cheese.
   Rale o queijo.
K. **Mix** the ingredients.
   Misture os ingredientes.
L. **Bake** at 350° for 45 minutes.
   Asse a 350º por 45 minutos.

Chicken soup   Sopa de galinha

M. **Cut up** the chicken.
   Corte o frango em pedaços.
N. **Peel** the carrots.
   Descasque / Raspe as cenouras.
O. **Slice** the carrots.
   Corte as cenouras em fatias.

P. **Boil** the chicken.
   Ferva o frango.
Q. **Add** the vegetables.
   Adicione os legumes.
R. **Simmer** for 1 hour.
   Cozinhe em fogo brando por 1 hora.

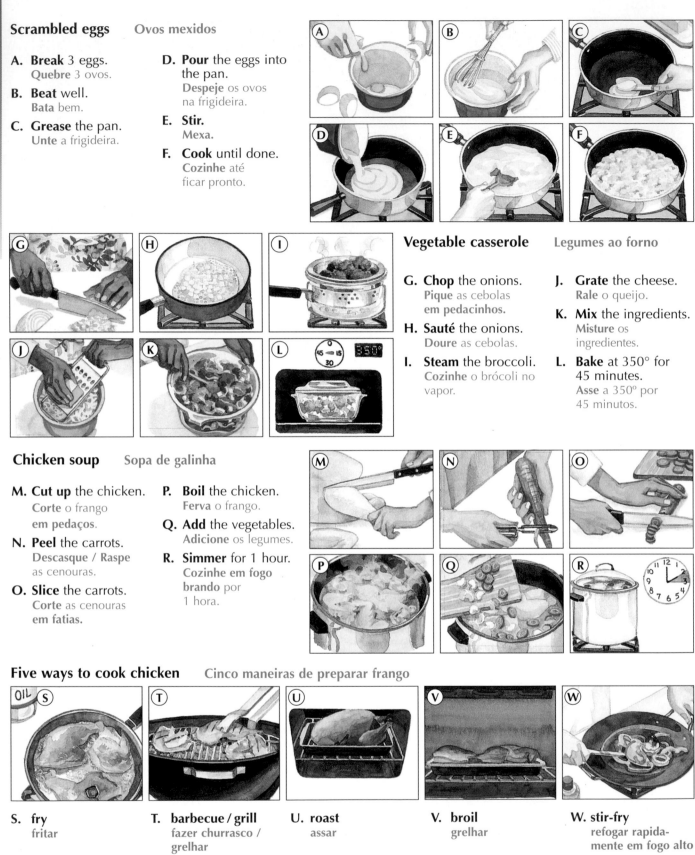

Five ways to cook chicken   Cinco maneiras de preparar frango

S. **fry**
   fritar
T. **barbecue / grill**
   fazer churrasco / grelhar
U. **roast**
   assar
V. **broil**
   grelhar
W. **stir-fry**
   refogar rapidamente em fogo alto

Talk about the way you prepare these foods.

I _fry_ eggs.

I _bake_ potatoes.

Share your answers.

1. What are popular ways in your country to make rice? vegetables? meat?
2. What is your favorite way to cook chicken?

1. **can opener**
   o abridor de latas

2. **grater**
   o ralador

3. **plastic storage container**
   os potes de plástico

4. **steamer**
   o escorredor para cozinhar a vapor

5. **frying pan**
   a frigideira

6. **pot**
   a panela / o caldeirão

7. **ladle**
   a concha

8. **double boiler**
   a panela para banho-maria

9. **wooden spoon**
   a colher de pau

10. **garlic press**
    o espremedor de alho

11. **casserole dish**
    a travessa refratária

12. **carving knife**
    a faca de trinchar

13. **roasting pan**
    a assadeira

14. **roasting rack**
    a grelha

15. **vegetable peeler**
    o descascador de legumes

16. **paring knife**
    a faca de descascar

17. **colander**
    o escorredor

18. **kitchen timer**
    o cronômetro para cozinha

19. **spatula**
    a espátula

20. **eggbeater**
    o batedor de ovos

21. **whisk**
    o batedor

22. **strainer**
    a peneira

23. **tongs**
    o pegador

24. **lid**
    a tampa

25. **saucepan**
    a panela

26. **cake pan**
    a assadeira para bolo

27. **cookie sheet**
    o tabuleiro para biscoito

28. **pie pan**
    a fôrma para torta

29. **pot holders**
    os pegadores de panela

30. **rolling pin**
    o rolo para massa / o pau de macarráo

31. **mixing bowl**
    a tigela

Talk about how to use the utensils.

You use a peeler to peel potatoes.

You use a pot to cook soup.

Use the new language.

Look at **Food Preparation**, page **58**.

Name the different utensils you see.

1. **hamburger**
   o hambúrguer

2. **french fries**
   as batatas fritas

3. **cheeseburger**
   o hambúrguer
   com queijo /
   o cheeseburger

4. **soda**
   o refrigerante

5. **iced tea**
   o chá gelado

6. **hot dog**
   o cachorro-quente

7. **pizza**
   a pizza

8. **green salad**
   a salada de verduras

9. **taco**
   o taco

10. **nachos**
    os nachos

11. **frozen yogurt**
    o frozen yogurt

12. **milk shake**
    o milk shake

13. **counter**
    o balcão

14. **muffin**
    o muffin (bolinho doce)

15. **doughnut**
    os donuts

16. **salad bar**
    o bufê de saladas

17. **lettuce**
    a alface

18. **salad dressing**
    o tempero / o molho
    para salada

19. **booth**
    a mesa

20. **straw**
    o canudinho

21. **sugar**
    o açúcar

22. **sugar substitute**
    o adoçante

23. **ketchup**
    o catchup

24. **mustard**
    a mostarda

25. **mayonnaise**
    a maionese

26. **relish**
    o picles

A. **eat**
   comer

B. **drink**
   beber

More vocabulary

donut: doughnut (spelling variation)

condiments: relish, mustard, ketchup, mayonnaise, etc.

Share your answers.

1. What would you order at this restaurant?

2. Which fast foods are popular in your country?

3. How often do you eat fast food? Why?

Breakfast

Lunch

Dinner

Desserts

Beverages

1. scrambled eggs
   os ovos mexidos

2. sausage
   a lingüiça

3. toast
   a torrada

4. waffles
   os waffles

5. syrup
   a calda

6. pancakes
   as panquecas

7. bacon
   o bacon

8. grilled cheese
   sandwich
   o sanduíche de queijo
   quente

9. chef's salad
   a salada à moda do chefe

10. soup of the day
    a sopa do dia

11. mashed potatoes
    o purê de batatas

12. roast chicken
    o frango assado

13. steak
    o filé / o bife

14. baked potato
    a batata assada

15. pasta
    o macarrão

16. garlic bread
    o pão de alho

17. fried fish
    o peixe frito

18. rice pilaf
    o arroz pilaf (oriental)

19. cake
    o bolo

20. pudding
    o pudim / o doce gelado

21. pie
    a torta

22. coffee
    o café

23. decaf coffee
    o café descafeinado

24. tea
    o chá

Practice ordering from the menu.

I'd like _a grilled cheese sandwich_ and _some soup_.

I'll have _the chef's salad_ and _a cup of decaf coffee_.

Use the new language.

Look at **Fruit,** page **50.**

Order a slice of pie using the different fruit flavors.

_Please give me a slice of _apple_ pie._

A Restaurant   Um restaurante

1. hostess
a recepcionista

2. dining room
o salão de refeições

3. menu
o cardápio / o menu

4. server / waiter
o garçom

5. patron / diner
o cliente / o freguês

A. set the table
por / arrumar a mesa

B. seat the customer
acompanhar um
cliente à mesa

C. pour the water
servir a água

D. order from the menu
fazer pedido do cardápio

E. take the order
anotar o pedido

F. serve the meal
servir a comida

G. clear the table
tirar a mesa

H. carry the tray
carregar a bandeja

I. pay the check
pagar a conta

J. leave a tip
deixar uma gorjeta

More vocabulary

eat out: to go to a restaurant to eat

take out: to buy food at a restaurant and take it home
to eat

Practice giving commands.

Please <u>set the table</u>.

I'd like you to <u>clear the table</u>.

It's time to <u>serve the meal</u>.

6. server / waitress
a garçonete

7. dessert tray
a bandeja de sobremesas

8. bread basket
a cesta de pães

9. busperson
o auxiliar de garçom

10. kitchen
a cozinha

11. chef
o chefe de cozinha / o
cozinheiro-chefe

12. dishroom
o recinto para lavar louça

13. dishwasher
o lavador de pratos

14. place setting
a arrumação da mesa

15. dinner plate
o prato raso

16. bread-and-butter plate
o prato para pão

17. salad plate
o prato para salada

18. soup bowl
o prato fundo / a tigela
para sopa

19. water glass
o copo para água

20. wine glass
a taça para vinho

21. cup
a xícara

22. saucer
o pires

23. napkin
o guardanapo

24. salad fork
o garfo para salada

25. dinner fork
o garfo para refeição

26. steak knife
a faca para carne

27. knife
a faca de mesa

28. teaspoon
a colher de chá

29. soupspoon
a colher de sopa

Talk about how you set the table in your home.

The glass is on the right.

The fork goes on the left.

The napkin is next to the plate.

Share your answers.

1. Do you know anyone who works in a restaurant?
What does he or she do?

2. In your opinion, which restaurant jobs are hard?
Why?

1. **three-piece suit**
   o terno completo (de três peças)

2. **suit**
   o tailleur / o conjunto

3. **dress**
   o vestido

4. **shirt**
   a camisa

5. **jeans**
   a calça jeans

6. **sports coat**
   o blazer / o paletó esporte

7. **turtleneck**
   o suéter de gola olímpica

8. **slacks / pants**
   a calça (social)

9. **blouse**
   a blusa

10. **skirt**
    a saia

11. **pullover sweater**
    o suéter

12. **T-shirt**
    a camiseta

13. **shorts**
    o short

14. **sweatshirt**
    o suéter de moletom

15. **sweatpants**
    a calça de moletom

More vocabulary:

outfit: clothes that look nice together

When clothes are popular, they are **in fashion.**

Talk about what you're wearing today and what you wore yesterday.

I'm wearing <u>a gray sweater</u>, <u>a red T-shirt</u>, and <u>blue jeans</u>.

Yesterday I wore <u>a green pullover sweater</u>, <u>a white shirt</u>, and <u>black slacks</u>.

16. jumpsuit	**21.** overalls	**26.** sports shirt
o macacão	o macacão	a camisa-esporte
17. uniform	**22.** tunic	**27.** cardigan sweater
o uniforme	a túnica	o cardigã
18. jumper	**23.** leggings	**28.** tuxedo
a jardineira	a calça fuseau	o smoking
19. maternity dress	**24.** vest	**29.** evening gown
o vestido para gestante	o colete	o vestido de noite
20. knit shirt	**25.** split skirt	
a camisa de malha	a saia-calça	

Use the new language.

Look at **A Graduation,** pages **32–33.**

Name the clothes you see.

The man at the podium is wearing a suit.

Share your answers.

1. Which clothes in this picture are in fashion now?

2. Who is the best-dressed person in this line? Why?

3. What do you wear when you go to the movies?

Clothing II   Vestuário II

1. **hat**
   o chapéu

2. **overcoat**
   o casaco / o sobretudo

3. **leather jacket**
   a jaqueta de couro

4. **wool scarf / muffler**
   o cachecol de lã

5. **gloves**
   as luvas

6. **cap**
   o boné

7. **jacket**
   a jaqueta

8. **parka**
   a jaqueta forrada com capuz / o anoraque

9. **mittens**
   a luva (com separação apenas para o polegar)

10. **ski cap**
    o gorro

11. **tights**
    a meia-calça

12. **earmuffs**
    o protetor para orelhas

13. **down vest**
    o colete acolchoado

14. **ski mask**
    a máscara de esqui / o gorro de esqui

15. **down jacket**
    a jaqueta acolchoada

16. **umbrella**
    o guarda-chuva

17. **raincoat**
    a capa de chuva

18. **poncho**
    o poncho

19. **rain boots**
    as galochas

20. **trench coat**
    a capa impermeável

21. **sunglasses**
    os óculos de sol

22. **swimming trunks**
    o calção de banho

23. **straw hat**
    o chapéu de palha

24. **windbreaker**
    o blusão esportivo

25. **cover-up**
    a saída-de-banho

26. **swimsuit / bathing suit**
    o maiô / o traje de banho

27. **baseball cap**
    o boné

Use the new language.

Look at **Weather,** page **10.**

Name the clothing for each weather condition.

Wear a jacket when it's windy.

Share your answers.

1. Which is better in the rain, an umbrella or a poncho?
2. Which is better in the cold, a parka or a down jacket?
3. Do you have more summer clothes or winter clothes?

1. leotard
a malha de ginástica

2. tank top
a camiseta-regata

3. bike shorts
o short de ciclista

4. pajamas
o pijama

5. nightgown
a camisola

6. slippers
os chinelos

7. blanket sleeper
o macacão de pezinho

8. bathrobe
o roupão

9. nightshirt
o camisolão /
o camisão de dormir

10. undershirt
a camiseta (de baixo)

11. long underwear
a roupa de baixo para inverno

12. boxer shorts
a cueca samba-canção

13. briefs
a cueca

14. athletic supporter / jockstrap
o suporte atlético / a sunga

15. socks
as meias

16. (bikini) panties
a calcinha cavada

17. briefs / underpants
a calcinha

18. girdle
a cinta elástica

19. garter belt
a cinta-liga

20. bra
o sutiã

21. camisole
a camisete / a mini-combinação

22. full slip
a combinação

23. half slip
a anágua

24. knee-highs
a meia 3/4 fina / de seda

25. kneesocks
a meia 3/4

26. stockings
a meia fina / de seda

27. pantyhose
a meia-calça fina / de seda

More vocabulary

lingerie: underwear or sleepwear for women

loungewear: clothing (sometimes sleepwear) people wear around the home

Share your answers.

1. What do you wear when you exercise?

2. What kind of clothing do you wear for sleeping?

Shoes and Accessories   Sapatos e acessórios

1. salesclerk
a vendedora

2. suspenders
os suspensórios

3. shoe department
a seção de calçados

4. silk scarves*
as echarpes de seda

5. hats
os chapéus

12. sole
a sola

13. heel
o salto

14. shoelace
o cadarço

15. toe
a ponta do sapato

16. pumps
o escarpin

17. high heels
o sapato de salto alto

18. boots
as botas

19. loafers
o mocassim

20. oxfords
o sapato de amarrar

21. hiking boots
as botas de montanhismo /
para caminhada

22. tennis shoes
o tênis

23. athletic shoes
o tênis esportivo

24. sandals
as sandálias

*****Note:** *one scarf, two scarves*

Talk about the shoes you're wearing today.
I'm wearing a pair of <u>white sandals</u>.

Practice asking a salesperson for help.
Could I try on these <u>sandals</u> in size <u>10</u>?
Do you have any <u>silk scarves</u>?
Where are <u>the hats</u>?

6. purses / handbags
as bolsas

7. display case
o balcão / o display

8. jewelry
as jóias e bijuterias

9. necklaces
os colares

10. ties
as gravatas

11. belts
os cintos

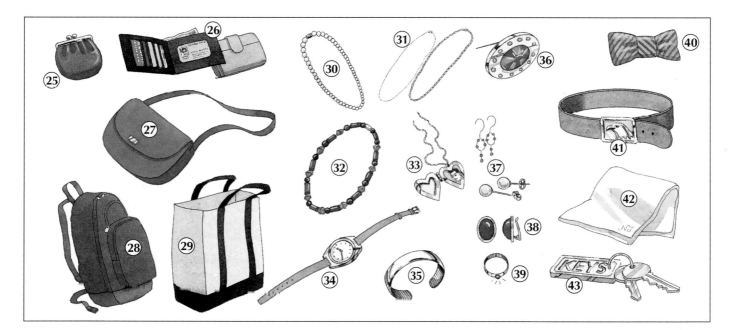

25. change purse
o porta-níqueis

26. wallet
a carteira

27. shoulder bag
a bolsa a tiracolo

28. backpack / bookbag
a mochila

29. tote bag
a sacola

30. string of pearls
o colar de pérolas

31. chain
a corrente

32. beads
as contas

33. locket
o medalhão
(tipo relicário)

34. (wrist)watch
o relógio de pulso

35. bracelet
a pulseira

36. pin
o broche

37. pierced earrings
os brincos de tarraxa

38. clip-on earrings
os brincos de pressão

39. ring
o anel

40. bow tie
a gravata-borboleta

41. belt buckle
a fivela do cinto

42. handkerchief
o lenço de bolso

43. key chain
o chaveiro

Share your answers.

1. Which of these accessories are usually worn by women? by men?

2. Which of these do you wear every day?

3. Which of these would you wear to a job interview? Why?

4. Which accessory would you like to receive as a present? Why?

Sizes Tamanhos

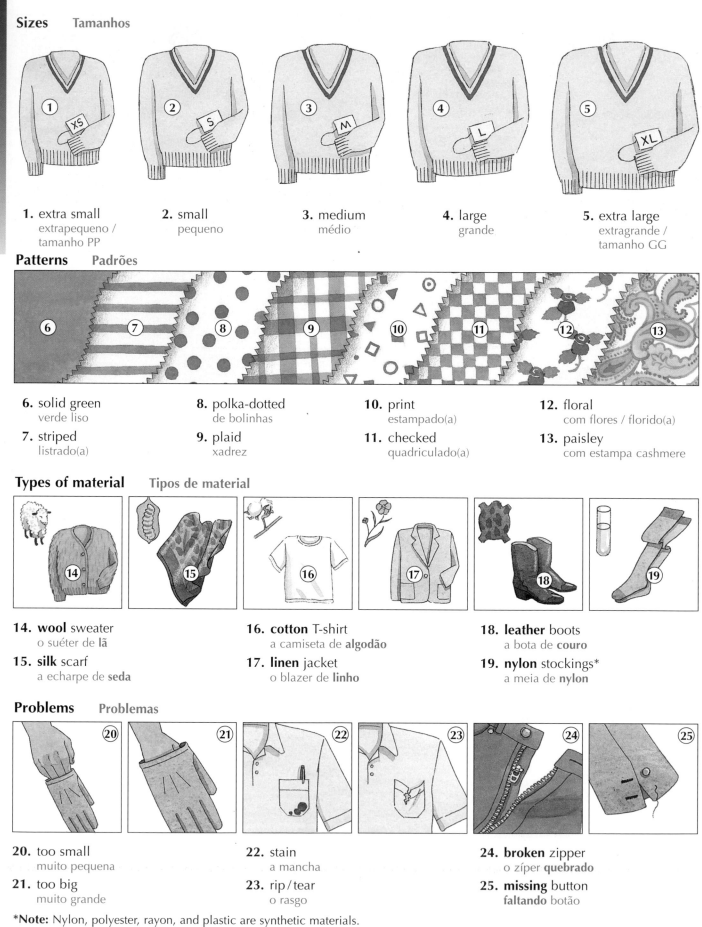

1. extra small
extrapequeno /
tamanho PP

2. small
pequeno

3. medium
médio

4. large
grande

5. extra large
extragrande /
tamanho GG

Patterns Padrões

6. solid green
verde liso

7. striped
listrado(a)

8. polka-dotted
de bolinhas

9. plaid
xadrez

10. print
estampado(a)

11. checked
quadriculado(a)

12. floral
com flores / florido(a)

13. paisley
com estampa cashmere

Types of material Tipos de material

14. wool sweater
o suéter de **lã**

15. silk scarf
a echarpe de **seda**

16. cotton T-shirt
a camiseta de **algodão**

17. linen jacket
o blazer de **linho**

18. leather boots
a bota de **couro**

19. nylon stockings*
a meia de **nylon**

Problems Problemas

20. too small
muito pequena

21. too big
muito grande

22. stain
a mancha

23. rip / tear
o rasgo

24. broken zipper
o zíper **quebrado**

25. missing button
faltando botão

***Note:** Nylon, polyester, rayon, and plastic are synthetic materials.

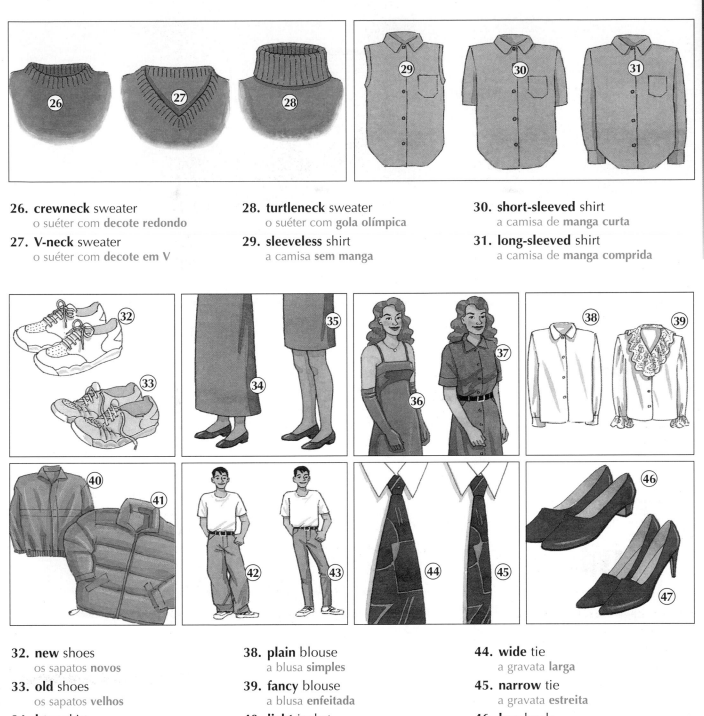

26. crewneck sweater
o suéter com **decote redondo**

27. V-neck sweater
o suéter com **decote em V**

28. turtleneck sweater
o suéter com **gola olímpica**

29. sleeveless shirt
a camisa **sem manga**

30. short-sleeved shirt
a camisa de **manga curta**

31. long-sleeved shirt
a camisa de **manga comprida**

32. new shoes
os sapatos **novos**

33. old shoes
os sapatos **velhos**

34. long skirt
a saia **longa**

35. short skirt
a saia **curta**

36. formal dress
o vestido de **festa**

37. casual dress
o vestido-**esporte**

38. plain blouse
a blusa **simples**

39. fancy blouse
a blusa **enfeitada**

40. light jacket
a jaqueta **leve / fina**

41. heavy jacket
a jaqueta **pesada / grossa**

42. loose pants / **baggy** pants
a calça **folgada / baggy**

43. tight pants
a calça **justa**

44. wide tie
a gravata **larga**

45. narrow tie
a gravata **estreita**

46. low heels
o salto **baixo**

47. high heels
o salto **alto**

Talk about yourself.

I like _long-sleeved_ shirts and _baggy_ pants.

I like _short skirts_ and _high heels_.

I usually wear _plain_ clothes.

Share your answers.

1. What type of material do you usually wear in the summer? in the winter?

2. What patterns do you see around you?

3. Are you wearing casual or formal clothes?

Doing the Laundry   Lavando roupa

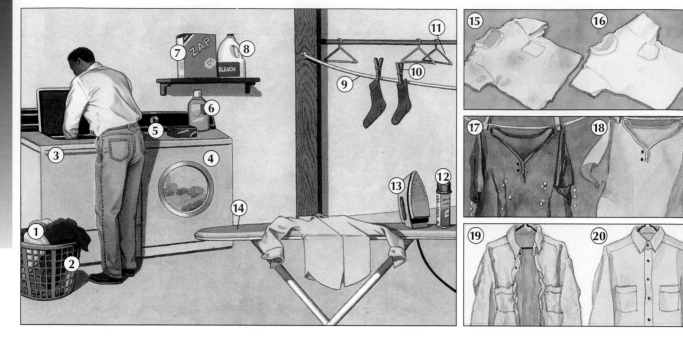

1. **laundry**
   a roupa suja

2. **laundry basket**
   o cesto de roupa suja

3. **washer**
   a máquina de lavar roupa

4. **dryer**
   a secadora de roupa

5. **dryer sheets**
   o papel-amaciante
   para secadora

6. **fabric softener**
   o amaciante de roupa

7. **laundry detergent**
   o sabão em pó

8. **bleach**
   o alvejante

9. **clothesline**
   o varal

10. **clothespin**
    o pregador (de roupas)

11. **hanger**
    o cabide

12. **spray starch**
    o spray para engomar

13. **iron**
    o ferro de passar

14. **ironing board**
    a tábua de passar roupa

15. **dirty** T-shirt
    a camiseta **suja**

16. **clean** T-shirt
    a camiseta **limpa**

17. **wet** T-shirt
    a camiseta **molhada**

18. **dry** T-shirt
    a camiseta **seca**

19. **wrinkled** shirt
    a camisa **amassada**

20. **ironed** shirt
    a camisa **passada**

A. **Sort** the laundry.
    Separe a roupa.

B. **Add** the detergent.
    Adicione o sabão.

C. **Load** the washer.
    Coloque a roupa na
    máquina de lavar.

D. **Clean** the lint trap.
    Limpe o filtro de fiapos.

E. **Unload** the dryer.
    Esvazie a secadora.

F. **Fold** the laundry.
    Dobre a roupa.

G. **Iron** the clothes.
    Passe a roupa.

H. **Hang up** the clothes.
    Pendure a roupa.

More vocabulary

dry cleaners: a business that cleans clothes using chemicals, not water and detergent

 wash in cold water only

 no bleach

 line dry

 dry-clean only, do not wash

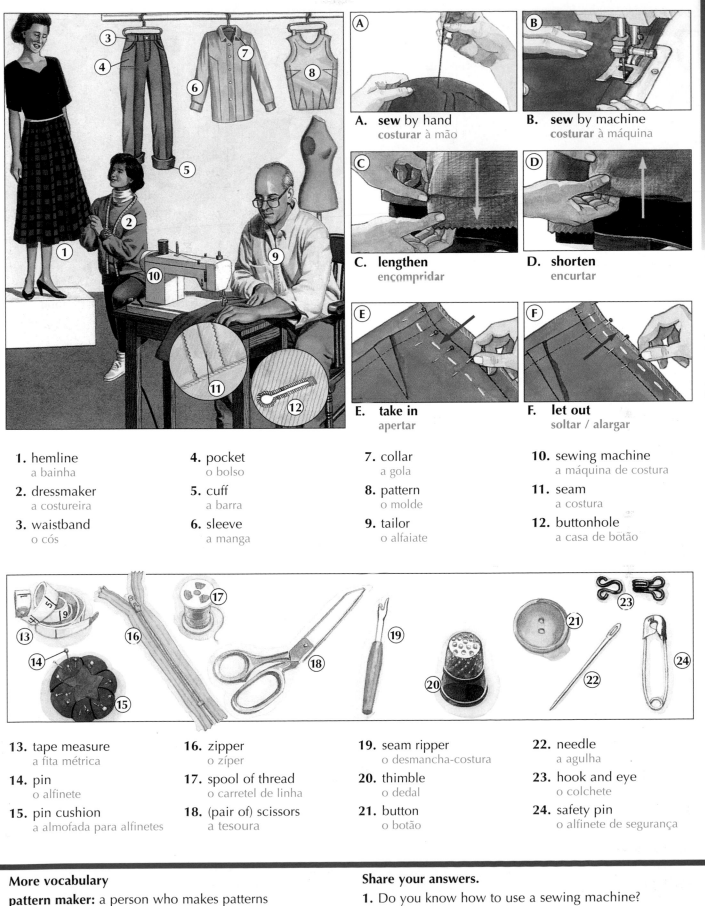

A. **sew** by hand
costurar à mão

B. **sew** by machine
costurar à máquina

C. **lengthen**
encompridar

D. **shorten**
encurtar

E. **take in**
apertar

F. **let out**
soltar / alargar

1. hemline
a bainha

2. dressmaker
a costureira

3. waistband
o cós

4. pocket
o bolso

5. cuff
a barra

6. sleeve
a manga

7. collar
a gola

8. pattern
o molde

9. tailor
o alfaiate

10. sewing machine
a máquina de costura

11. seam
a costura

12. buttonhole
a casa de botão

13. tape measure
a fita métrica

14. pin
o alfinete

15. pin cushion
a almofada para alfinetes

16. zipper
o zíper

17. spool of thread
o carretel de linha

18. (pair of) scissors
a tesoura

19. seam ripper
o desmancha-costura

20. thimble
o dedal

21. button
o botão

22. needle
a agulha

23. hook and eye
o colchete

24. safety pin
o alfinete de segurança

More vocabulary

pattern maker: a person who makes patterns

garment worker: a person who works in a clothing factory

fashion designer: a person who makes original clothes

Share your answers.

1. Do you know how to use a sewing machine?

2. Can you sew by hand?

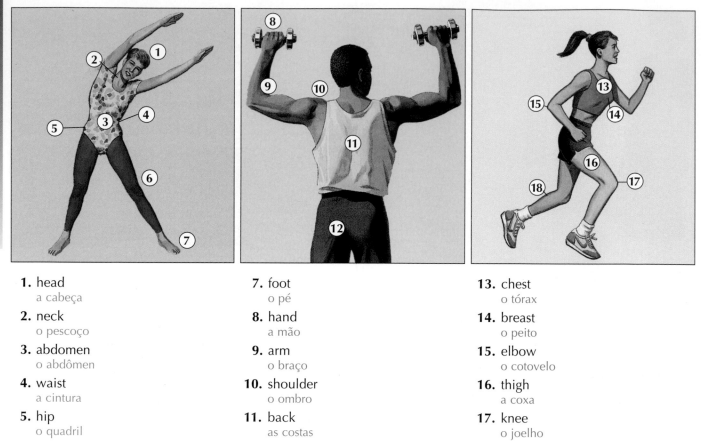

1. head a cabeça	**7.** foot o pé	**13.** chest o tórax
2. neck o pescoço	**8.** hand a mão	**14.** breast o peito
3. abdomen o abdômen	**9.** arm o braço	**15.** elbow o cotovelo
4. waist a cintura	**10.** shoulder o ombro	**16.** thigh a coxa
5. hip o quadril	**11.** back as costas	**17.** knee o joelho
6. leg a perna	**12.** buttocks as nádegas	**18.** calf a barriga da perna / a panturrilha

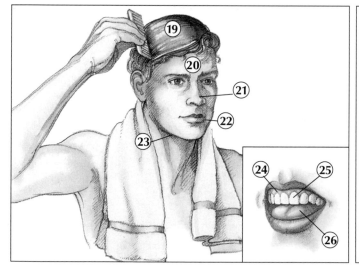

The face
O rosto

19. hair o cabelo	**23.** jaw a mandíbula	**27.** eye o olho	**32.** eyebrow a sobrancelha
20. forehead a testa	**24.** gums a gengiva	**28.** ear a orelha	**33.** eyelid a pálpebra
21. nose o nariz	**25.** teeth os dentes	**29.** cheek a bochecha	**34.** eyelashes os cílios
22. mouth a boca	**26.** tongue a língua	**30.** lip o lábio	
		31. chin o queixo	

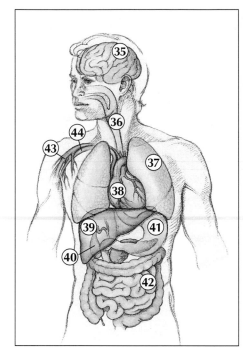

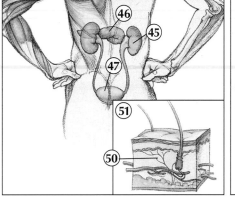

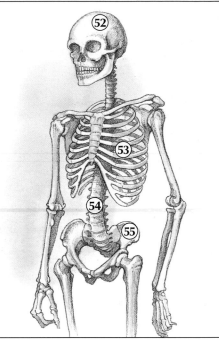

Inside the body
Dentro do corpo

35. brain
o cérebro

36. throat
a garganta

37. lung
o pulmão

38. heart
o coração

39. liver
o fígado

40. gallbladder
a vesícula biliar

41. stomach
o estômago

42. intestines
o intestino

43. artery
a artéria

44. vein
a veia

45. kidney
o rim

46. pancreas
o pâncreas

47. bladder
a bexiga

48. muscle
o músculo

49. bone
o osso

50. nerve
o nervo

51. skin
a pele

The skeleton
O esqueleto

52. skull
o crânio

53. rib cage
a caixa torácica

54. spinal column
a coluna vertebral

55. pelvis
a pélvis

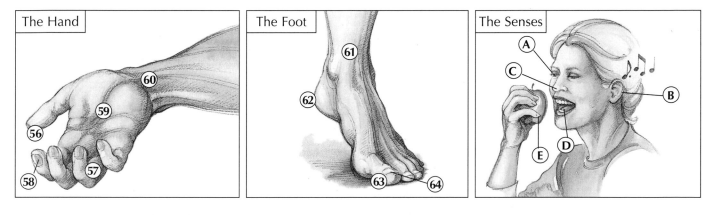

56. thumb
o polegar

57. fingers
os dedos (da mão)

58. fingernail
a unha (da mão)

59. palm
a palma (da mão)

60. wrist
o pulso / a munheca

61. ankle
o tornozelo

62. heel
o calcanhar

63. toe
o dedo (do pé)

64. toenail
a unha (do pé)

A. **see**
ver

B. **hear**
ouvir

C. **smell**
cheirar / sentir o cheiro

D. **taste**
sentir o gosto

E. **touch**
tocar

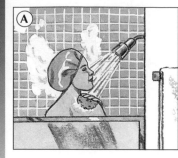

A. take a shower
tomar banho
(de chuveiro)

B. bathe / take a bath
tomar banho
(de banheira)

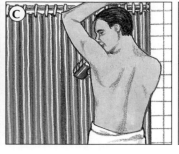

C. use deodorant
passar desodorante

D. put on sunscreen
passar protetor solar

1. shower cap
a touca de banho

2. soap
o sabonete

3. bath powder / talcum powder
o talco

4. deodorant
o desodorante

5. perfume / cologne
o perfume / a colônia

6. sunscreen
o protetor solar

7. body lotion
o hidratante para o corpo

8. moisturizer
o (creme) hidratante

E. wash…hair
lavar o cabelo

F. rinse…hair
enxaguar
o cabelo

G. comb…hair
pentear
o cabelo

H. dry…hair
secar
o cabelo

I. brush…hair
escovar
o cabelo

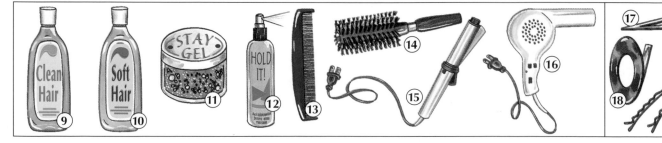

9. shampoo
o shampoo

10. conditioner
o condicionador

11. hair gel
o gel para cabelo ·

12. hair spray
o laquê / o fixador
de cabelo

13. comb
o pente

14. brush
a escova

15. curling iron
o modelador de cabelo

16. blow dryer
o secador de cabelo

17. hair clip
o clipe para cabelo

18. barrette
a fivela

19. bobby pins
os grampos

J. brush...teeth
escovar os dentes

K. floss...teeth
passar fio dental

L. gargle
fazer gargarejo

M. shave
barbear-se

20. toothbrush
a escova de dente

21. toothpaste
a pasta de dente

22. dental floss
o fio dental

23. mouthwash
o anti-séptico bucal

24. electric shaver
o barbeador elétrico

25. razor
o aparelho de barbear

26. razor blade
a lâmina de barbear

27. shaving cream
o creme de barbear

28. aftershave
a loção após barba

N. cut...nails
cortar as unhas

O. polish...nails
pintar as unhas

P. put on...makeup
maquiar-se

29. nail clipper
o cortador de unha

30. emery board
a lixa de unha

31. nail polish
o esmalte

32. nail polish remover
a acetona / o removedor
de esmalte

33. eyebrow pencil
o lápis de sobrancelhas

34. eye shadow
a sombra

35. eyeliner
o delineador

36. blush / rouge
o blush

37. lipstick
o batom

38. mascara
o rímel

39. face powder
o pó facial

40. foundation
a base

More vocabulary

A product without perfume or scent is **unscented.**

A product that is better for people with allergies is
hypoallergenic.

Share your answers.

1. What is your morning routine if you stay home?
if you go out?

2. Do women in your culture wear makeup? How old
are they when they begin to use it?

1. **headache**
   a dor de cabeça

2. **toothache**
   a dor de dente

3. **earache**
   a dor de ouvido

4. **stomachache**
   a dor de estômago

5. **backache**
   a dor nas costas

6. **sore throat**
   a dor de garganta

7. **nasal congestion**
   a congestão nasal

8. **fever / temperature**
   a febre

9. **chills**
   os calafrios

10. **rash**
    a erupção / a irritação cutânea

A. **cough**
   tossir

B. **sneeze**
   espirrar

C. **feel** dizzy
   sentir-se tonto

D. **feel** nauseous
   sentir náuseas

E. **throw up / vomit**
   vomitar

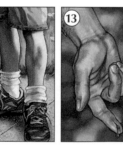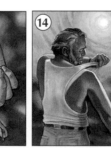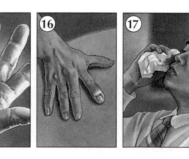

11. **insect bite**
    a picada de inseto

12. **bruise**
    a contusão

13. **cut**
    o corte

14. **sunburn**
    a queimadura de sol

15. **blister**
    a bolha

16. **swollen** finger
    o dedo **inchado**

17. **bloody** nose
    o **sangramento** do nariz

18. **sprained** ankle
    o tornozelo **torcido**

Use the new language.

Look at **Health Care,** pages 80–81.

Tell what medication or treatment you would use for each health problem.

Share your answers.

1. For which problems would you go to a doctor? use medication? do nothing?

2. What do you do for a sunburn? for a headache?

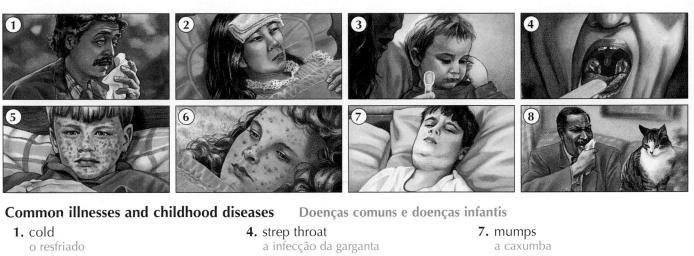

Common illnesses and childhood diseases   Doenças comuns e doenças infantis

1. cold
o resfriado

2. flu
a gripe

3. ear infection
a infecção do ouvido

4. strep throat
a infecção da garganta

5. measles
o sarampo

6. chicken pox
a catapora

7. mumps
a caxumba

8. allergies
as alergias

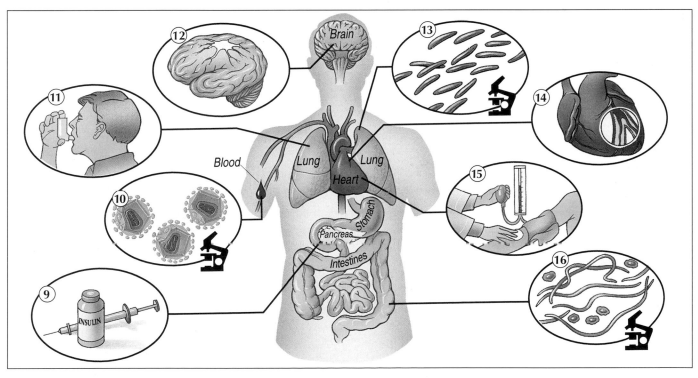

Medical conditions and serious diseases   Problemas crônicos de saúde e doenças graves

9. diabetes
a diabete

10. HIV (human immunodeficiency virus)
o HIV (vírus da imunodeficiência humana)

11. asthma
a asma

12. brain cancer
o câncer do cérebro

13. TB (tuberculosis)
a tuberculose

14. heart disease
a doença cardíaca

15. high blood pressure
a pressão alta

16. intestinal parasites
os parasitas intestinais

More vocabulary

AIDS (acquired immunodeficiency syndrome): a medical condition that results from contracting the HIV virus

influenza: flu

hypertension: high blood pressure

infectious disease: a disease that is spread through air or water

Share your answers.

Which diseases on this page are infectious?

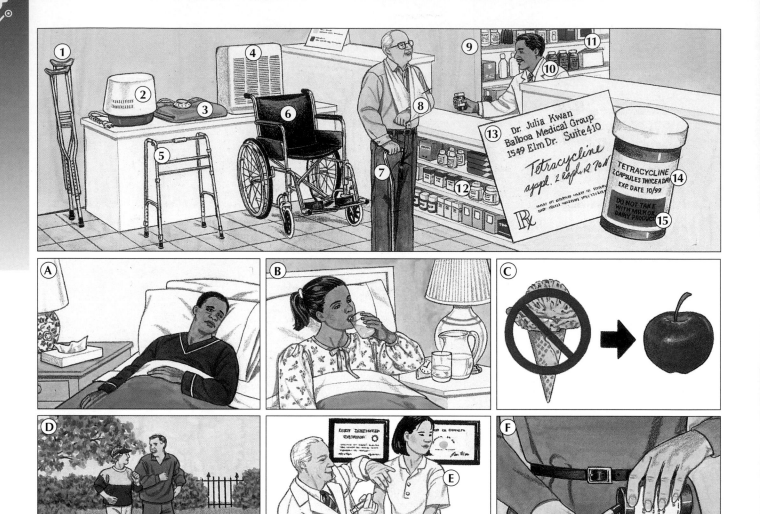

1. **crutches**
   as muletas

2. **humidifier**
   o vaporizador

3. **heating pad**
   a almofada térmica

4. **air purifier**
   o purificador de ar

5. **walker**
   o andador

6. **wheelchair**
   a cadeira de rodas

7. **cane**
   a bengala

8. **sling**
   a tipóia

9. **pharmacy**
   a farmácia

10. **pharmacist**
    o farmacêutico

11. **prescription medication**
    o medicamento com receita médica

12. **over-the-counter medication**
    o medicamento sem receita médica

13. **prescription**
    a receita médica

14. **prescription label**
    o rótulo da receita médica

15. **warning label**
    o rótulo de precauções

A. **Get** bed rest.
   Faça repouso.

B. **Drink** fluids.
   Tome líquidos.

C. **Change** your diet.
   Mude sua dieta.

D. **Exercise.**
   Faça exercícios.

E. **Get** an injection.
   Tome uma injeção.

F. **Take** medicine.
   Tome remédio.

More vocabulary

dosage: how much medicine you take and how many times a day you take it

expiration date: the last day the medicine can be used

treatment: something you do to get better

Staying in bed, drinking fluids, and getting physical therapy are treatments.

An injection that stops a person from getting a serious disease is called **an immunization** or **a vaccination.**

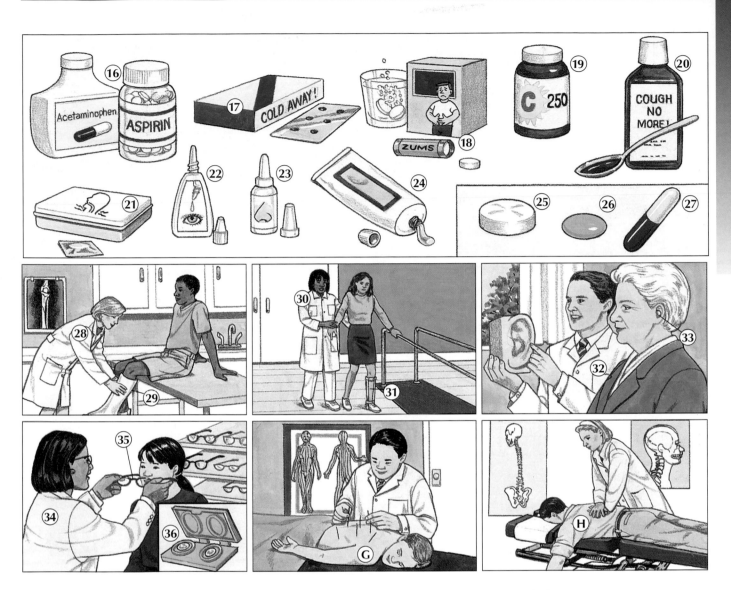

16. pain reliever o analgésico	**24.** ointment a pomada	**32.** audiologist o audiologista
17. cold tablets os comprimidos para resfriado	**25.** tablet o comprimido	**33.** hearing aid o aparelho auditivo
18. antacid o antiácido	**26.** pill a pílula	**34.** optometrist a optometrista
19. vitamins as vitaminas	**27.** capsule a cápsula	**35.** (eye)glasses os óculos
20. cough syrup o xarope para tosse	**28.** orthopedist a ortopedista	**36.** contact lenses as lentes de contato
21. throat lozenges as pastilhas para garganta	**29.** cast o gesso	**G. Get** acupuncture. **Faça** acupuntura.
22. eyedrops o colírio	**30.** physical therapist a fisioterapeuta	**H. Go** to a chiropractor. **Vá** a um quiroprático.
23. nasal spray o spray nasal	**31.** brace o aparelho ortopédico (órtese)	

Share your answers.

1. What's the best treatment for a headache? a sore throat? a stomachache? a fever?

2. Do you think vitamins are important? Why or why not?

3. What treatments are popular in your culture?

A. **be injured / be hurt**
machucar-se / ferir-se

B. **be** unconscious
estar inconsciente / **estar** desmaiada

C. **be** in shock
estar em choque

D. **have** a heart attack
ter um ataque do coração

E. **have** an allergic reaction
ter uma reação alérgica

F. **get** an electric shock
receber um choque elétrico

G. **get** frostbite
queimar-se por congelamento

H. **burn** (your)self
queimar(-se)

I. **drown**
afogar-se

J. **swallow** poison
ingerir veneno

K. **overdose** on drugs
tomar dose excessiva de
drogas / medicamentos

L. **choke**
engasgar-se / asfixiar-se

M. **bleed**
sangrar

N. **can't breathe**
asfixiar-se

O. **fall**
cair

P. **break** a bone
quebrar um osso

Grammar point: past tense

burn	—	burned	choke — choked	bleed	— bled
drown	—	drowned	be — was, were	can't	— couldn't
swallow	—	swallowed	have — had	fall	— fell
overdose	—	overdosed	get — got	break	— broke

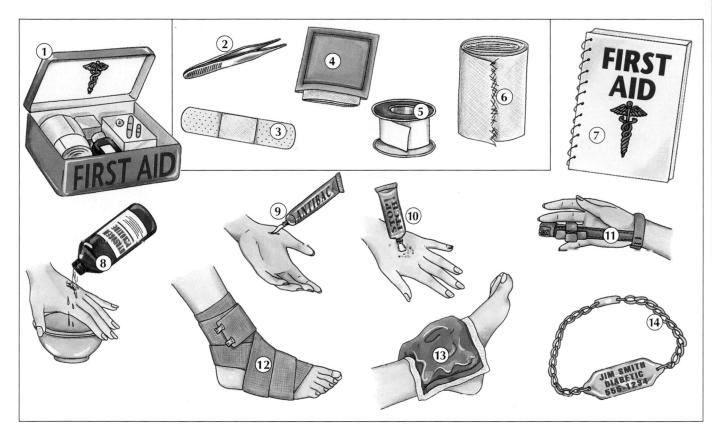

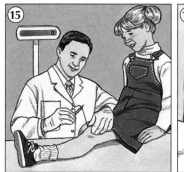

1. **first aid kit**
   o kit / o estojo de primeiros socorros

2. **tweezers**
   a pinça

3. **adhesive bandage**
   o curativo anti-séptico auto-adesivo

4. **sterile pad**
   o curativo esterilizado

5. **tape**
   o esparadrapo

6. **gauze**
   a gaze

7. **first aid manual**
   o manual de primeiros socorros

8. **hydrogen peroxide**
   a água oxigenada

9. **antibacterial ointment**
   a pomada antibacteriana

10. **antihistamine cream**
    o creme anti-histamínico

11. **splint**
    a tala

12. **elastic bandage**
    a atadura elástica

13. **ice pack**
    a bolsa de gelo

14. **medical emergency bracelet**
    a pulseira de emergência médica

15. **stitches**
    os pontos

16. **rescue breathing**
    a respiração boca-a-boca

17. **CPR (cardiopulmonary resuscitation)**
    o ressuscitamento cardiopulmonar

18. **Heimlich maneuver**
    a manobra de Heimlich

Important Note: Only people who are properly trained should give stitches or do CPR.

Share your answers.

1. Do you have a First Aid kit in your home? Where can you buy one?

2. When do you use hydrogen peroxide? an elastic support bandage? antihistamine cream?

3. Do you know first aid? Where did you learn it?

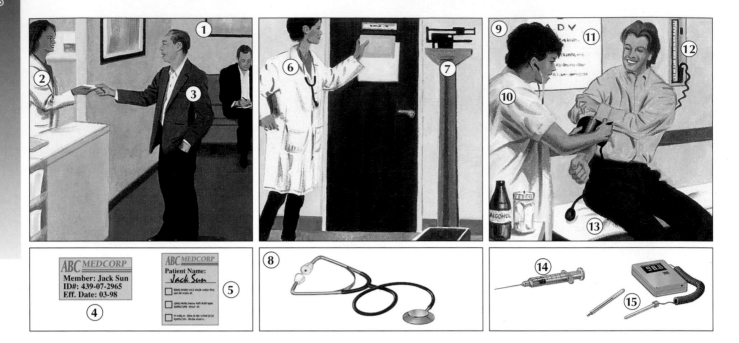

Medical clinic   Consultório médico

1. waiting room
a sala de espera

2. receptionist
a recepcionista

3. patient
o paciente

4. insurance card
o cartão de seguro-saúde

5. insurance form
o formulário do seguro-saúde

6. doctor
a médica

7. scale
a balança

8. stethoscope
o estetoscópio

9. examining room
a sala de exame

10. nurse
a enfermeira

11. eye chart
o quadro para exame da vista

12. blood pressure gauge
o aparelho de medir pressão /
o manômetro

13. examination table
a mesa de exame

14. syringe
a seringa

15. thermometer
o termômetro

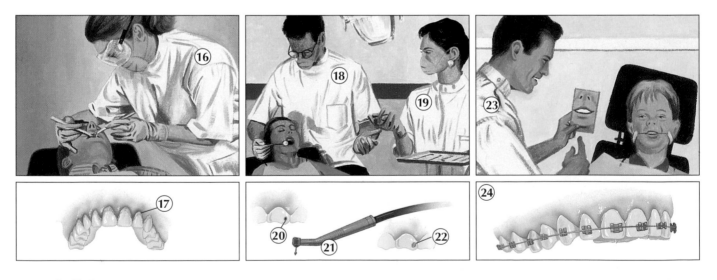

Dental clinic   Consultório dentário

16. dental hygienist
a técnica em higiene bucal

17. tartar
o tártaro

18. dentist
o dentista

19. dental assistant
a auxiliar de dentista

20. cavity
a cárie

21. drill
a broca

22. filling
a obturação / a restauração

23. orthodontist
o ortodontista

24. braces
o aparelho ortodôntico

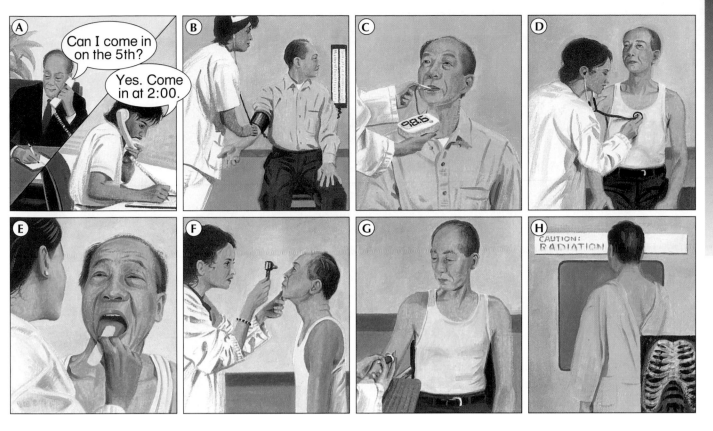

A. **make** an appointment
   marcar hora

B. **check**…blood pressure
   verificar a pressão sangüínea

C. **take**…temperature
   tirar a temperatura

D. **listen** to…heart
   auscultar o coração

E. **look** in…throat
   examinar a garganta

F. **examine**…eyes
   examinar os olhos

G. **draw**…blood
   tirar sangue

H. **get** an X ray
   tirar um Raio X

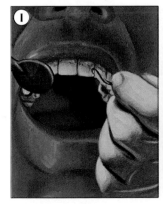

I. **clean**…teeth
   limpar os dentes

J. **give**…a shot of anesthetic
   dar (uma injeção de) anestesia

K. **drill** a tooth
   perfurar um dente com a broca

L. **fill** a cavity
   fazer uma obturação

M. **pull** a tooth
   arrancar / extrair um dente

More vocabulary

get a checkup: to go for a medical exam

extract a tooth: to pull out a tooth

Share your answers.

1. What is the average cost of a medical exam in your area?

2. Some people are nervous at the dentist's office. What can they do to relax?

A Hospital   Um hospital

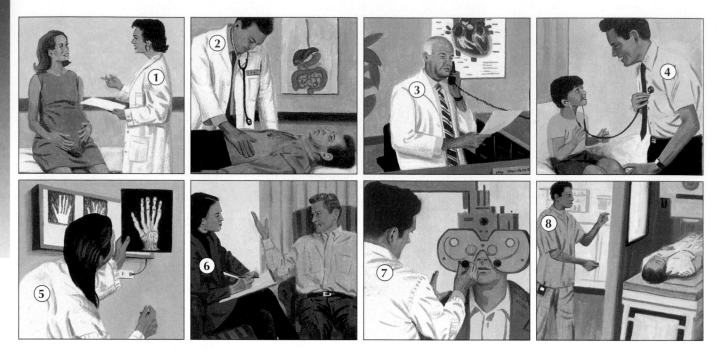

Hospital staff   A equipe do hospital

1. obstetrician
a obstetra

2. internist
o clínico geral

3. cardiologist
o cardiologista

4. pediatrician
o pediatra

5. radiologist
a radiologista

6. psychiatrist
a psiquiatra

7. ophthalmologist
o oftalmologista

8. X-ray technician
o técnico de radiologia

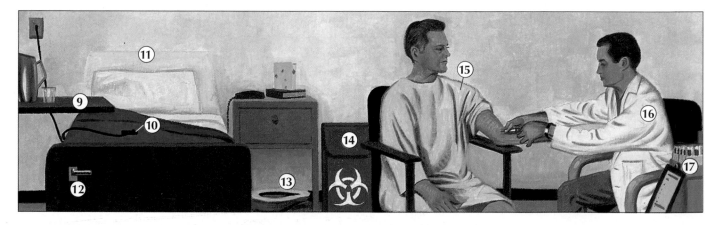

Patient's room   O quarto do paciente

9. bed table
a mesa de cama

10. call button
a campainha

11. hospital bed
a cama hospitalar

12. bed control
o controle da cama / a manivela

13. bedpan
a comadre

14. medical waste disposal
o recipiente para lixo hospitalar

15. hospital gown
a camisola hospitalar

16. lab technician
o técnico de laboratório

17. blood work / blood test
o exame de sangue

More vocabulary

nurse practitioner: a nurse licensed to give medical exams

specialist: a doctor who only treats specific medical problems

gynecologist: a specialist who examines and treats women

nurse midwife: a nurse practitioner who examines pregnant women and delivers babies

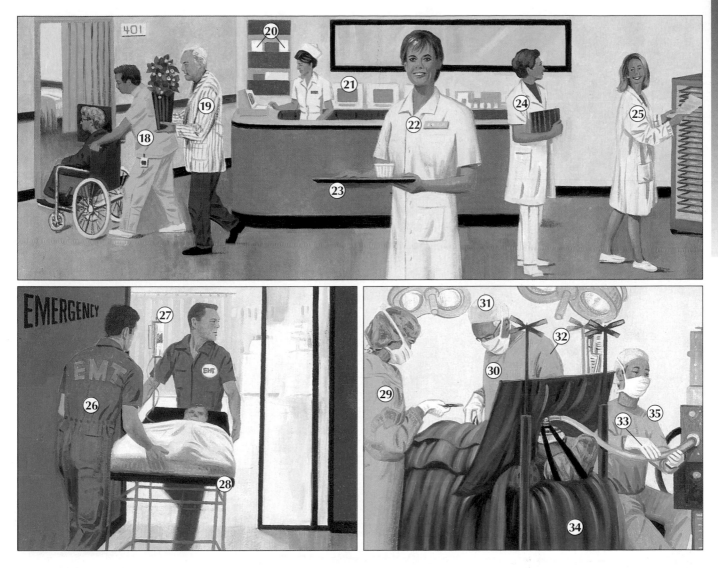

Nurse's station
Balcão de enfermagem

18. orderly
o atendente / o auxiliar
de enfermagem

19. volunteer
o voluntário

20. medical charts
o prontuário médico

21. vital signs monitor
o monitor de sinais vitais

22. RN (registered nurse)
a enfermeira-padrão

23. medication tray
a bandeja de medicamentos

24. LPN (licensed practical nurse) /
LVN (licensed vocational nurse)
a técnica em enfermagem

25. dietician
a nutricionista

Emergency room
**Pronto Atendimento /
Pronto-Socorro**

26. emergency medical technician
(EMT)
o socorrista / o técnico em
emergência

27. IV (intravenous drip)
o soro intravenoso

28. stretcher / gurney
a maca

Operating room
Sala de cirurgia

29. surgical nurse
a instrumentadora / a enfermeira
cirúrgica

30. surgeon
o cirurgião

31. surgical cap
a touca de cirurgião

32. surgical gown
o avental de cirurgião

33. latex gloves
as luvas cirúrgicas

34. operating table
a mesa de operação

35. anesthesiologist
o anestesista

Practice asking for the hospital staff.

Please get the nurse. I have a question for her.

Where's the anesthesiologist? I need to talk to her.

I'm looking for the lab technician. Have you seen him?

Share your answers.

1. Have you ever been to an emergency room? Who helped you?

2. Have you ever been in the hospital? How long did you stay?

87

1. **fire station**
   o posto do corpo de bombeiros

2. **coffee shop**
   a lanchonete

3. **bank**
   o banco

4. **car dealership**
   a concessionária de automóveis

5. **hotel**
   o hotel

6. **church**
   a igreja

7. **hospital**
   o hospital

8. **park**
   o parque

9. **synagogue**
   a sinagoga

10. **theater**
    o teatro

11. **movie theater**
    o cinema

12. **gas station**
    o posto de gasolina

13. **furniture store**
    a loja de móveis

14. **hardware store**
    a loja de ferragens

15. **barber shop**
    a barbearia

More vocabulary

skyscraper: a very tall office building

downtown / city center: the area in a city with the city hall, courts, and businesses

Practice giving your destination.

I'm going to go downtown.

I have to go to the post office.

16. bakery
a padaria

17. city hall
a prefeitura

18. courthouse
o fórum

19. police station
a delegacia de polícia

20. market
o supermercado

21. health club
a academia de ginástica

22. motel
o motel

23. mosque
a mesquita

24. office building
o prédio de escritórios

25. high-rise building
o arranha-céu

26. parking garage
o estacionamento

27. school
a escola

28. library
a biblioteca

29. post office
o correio

Practice asking for and giving the locations of buildings.

Where's the post office?

It's on Oak Street.

Share your answers.

1. Which of the places in this picture do you go to every week?

2. Is it good to live in a city? Why or why not?

3. What famous cities do you know?

89

A Mall   Um shopping center

1. music store
   a loja de discos

2. jewelry store
   a joalheria

3. candy store
   a doceria

4. bookstore
   a livraria

5. toy store
   a loja de brinquedos

6. pet store
   a loja de animais

7. card store
   a loja de cartões

8. optician
   a óptica

9. travel agency
   a agência de viagens

10. shoe store
    a loja de calçados

11. fountain
    a fonte

12. florist
    a floricultura

More vocabulary

beauty shop: hair salon

men's store: a store that sells men's clothing

dress shop: a store that sells women's clothing

Talk about where you want to shop in this mall.

Let's go to the card store.

I need to buy a card for Maggie's birthday.

13. department store
    a loja de departamentos

14. food court
    a praça de alimentação

15. video store
    a loja de vídeos

16. hair salon
    o salão de beleza

17. maternity shop
    a loja de artigos para gestantes

18. electronics store
    a loja de artigos eletrônicos

19. directory
    o painel de informações

20. ice cream stand
    o quiosque de sorvete

21. escalator
    a escada rolante

22. information booth
    o balcão de informações

Practice asking for and giving the location of different shops.

Where's <u>the maternity shop</u>?

  It's on <u>the first floor</u>, next to <u>the hair salon.</u>

Share your answers.

1. Do you like shopping malls? Why or why not?
2. Some people don't go to the mall to shop.
   Name some other things you can do in a mall.

A Childcare Center   Uma escolinha infantil / creche

1. parent
o pai / a mãe

2. stroller
o carrinho de bebê

3. childcare worker
a funcionária da escolinha

4. cubby
o armário de escaninhos

5. toys
os brinquedos

6. rocking chair
a cadeira de balanço

A. drop off
deixar

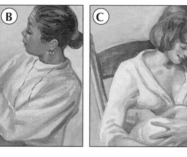

B. hold
segurar

C. nurse
amamentar

D. feed
alimentar

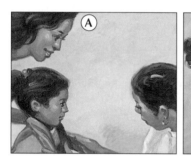

E. change diapers
trocar as fraldas

F. read a story
ler uma história

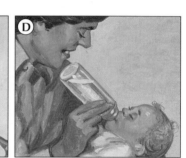

G. pick up
pegar no colo

H. rock
balançar

I. tie shoes
amarrar os sapatos

J. dress
vestir

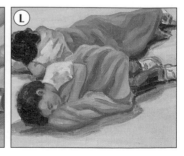

K. play
brincar

L. take a nap
tirar uma soneca

7. high chair
o cadeirão

8. bib
o babador

9. changing table
o trocador

10. potty seat
o piniquinho

11. playpen
o cercadinho

12. walker
o andador

13. car safety seat
a cadeira para automóvel

14. baby carrier
o bebê-conforto

15. baby backpack
o carregador de bebê

16. carriage
o carrinho de bebê

17. wipes
os lenços umedecidos

18. baby powder
o talco para bebê

19. disinfectant
o desinfetante

20. disposable diapers
as fraldas descartáveis

21. cloth diapers
as fraldas de pano

22. diaper pins
os alfinetes de fraldas

23. diaper pail
o cesto de fraldas

24. training pants
a fralda-calça

25. formula
o leite em pó infantil

26. bottle
a mamadeira

27. nipple
o bico da mamadeira

28. baby food
o alimento infantil

29. pacifier
a chupeta

30. teething ring
o mordedor

31. rattle
o chocalho

1. **envelope**
   o envelope

2. **letter**
   o carta

3. **postcard**
   o cartão-postal

4. **greeting card**
   o cartão

5. **package**
   o pacote

6. **letter carrier**
   a carteira

7. **return address**
   o endereço do remetente

8. **mailing address**
   o endereço do
   destinatário

9. **postmark**
   o carimbo

10. **stamp / postage**
    o selo / a franquia (postal)

11. **certified mail**
    a carta registrada

12. **priority mail**
    a encomenda expressa

13. **air letter / aerogramme**
    o aerograma

14. **ground post /
    parcel post**
    a encomenda normal
    (via terrestre)

15. **Express Mail /
    overnight mail**
    a encomenda expressa
    tipo sedex

A. **address** a postcard
   endereçar um cartão
   postal

B. **send** it / **mail** it
   **enviar / colocar no
   correio**

C. **deliver** it
   entregar

D. **receive** it
   receber

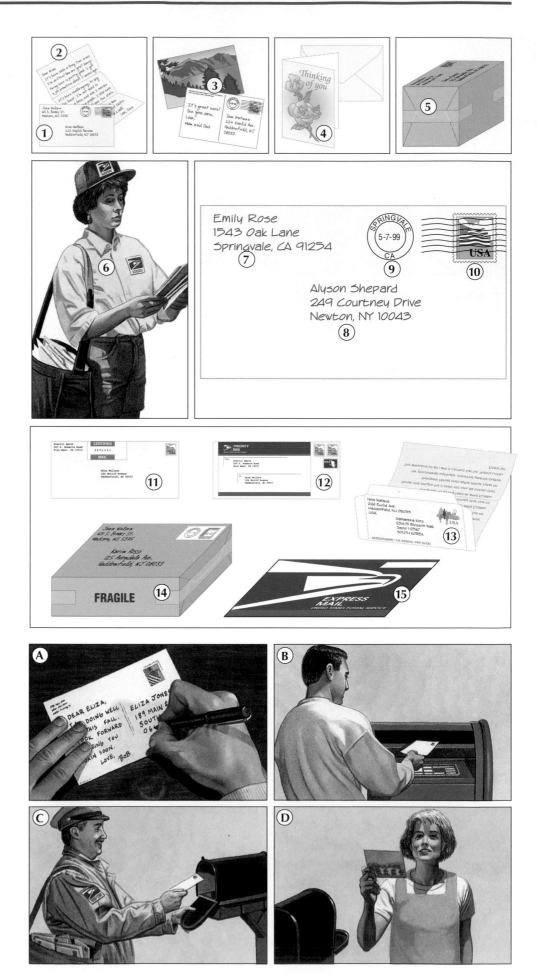

1. teller
   o caixa
2. vault
   o cofre
3. ATM (automated teller machine)
   o caixa automático
4. security guard
   o segurança

5. passbook
   o controle de saques e depósitos
6. savings account number
   o número da conta de poupança
7. checkbook
   o talão de cheques
8. checking account number
   o número da conta corrente
9. ATM card
   o cartão magnético
10. monthly statement
    o extrato mensal
11. balance
    o saldo
12. deposit slip
    o comprovante de depósito
13. safe-deposit box
    a caixa de segurança / o cofre particular no banco

Using the ATM machine   Uso do caixa automático

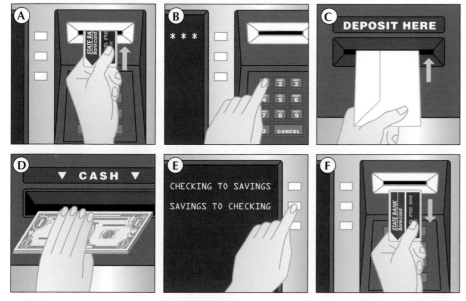

A. **Insert** your ATM card.
   Introduza seu cartão.
B. **Enter** your PIN number.*
   Digite sua senha.
C. **Make** a deposit.
   Faça um depósito.

D. **Withdraw** cash.
   Saque dinheiro.
E. **Transfer** funds.
   Transfira fundos.
F. **Remove** your ATM card.
   Retire seu cartão.

*PIN: personal identification number

More vocabulary

overdrawn account: When there is not enough money in an account to pay a check, we say the account is overdrawn.

Share your answers.

1. Do you use a bank?
2. Do you use an ATM card?
3. Name some things you can put in a safe-deposit box.

1. **reference librarian**
   a bibliotecária

2. **reference desk**
   o balcão de consulta

3. **atlas**
   o atlas

4. **microfilm reader**
   o leitor de microfilmes

5. **microfilm**
   os microfilmes

6. **periodical section**
   a seção de periódicos

7. **magazine**
   a revista

8. **newspaper**
   o jornal

9. **online catalog**
   o catálogo on-line

10. **card catalog**
    o fichário

11. **media section**
    a seção de audiovisuais

12. **audiocassette**
    a fita cassete

13. **videocassette**
    a fita de vídeo

14. **CD (compact disc)**
    o CD

15. **record**
    o disco

16. **checkout desk**
    o balcão de retirada

17. **library clerk**
    a funcionária da biblioteca

18. **encyclopedia**
    a enciclopédia

19. **library card**
    o cartão / a carteirinha da biblioteca

20. **library book**
    o livro da biblioteca

21. **title**
    o título

22. **author**
    a autora

More vocabulary

check a book out: to borrow a book from the library

nonfiction: real information, history or true stories

fiction: stories from the author's imagination

Share your answers.

1. Do you have a library card?

2. Do you prefer to buy books or borrow them from the library?

"You have the right to remain silent…"

"Bail is set at $20,000."

A. arrest a suspect
prender um suspeito

1. police officer
o policial

2. handcuffs
as algemas

B. hire a lawyer / **hire** an attorney
contratar um advogado

3. guard
o guarda

4. defense attorney
o advogado de defesa

C. appear in court
comparecer ao tribunal

5. defendant
o réu / o acusado

6. judge
o juiz

D. stand trial
ser julgado

7. courtroom
a sala do tribunal

8. jury
o júri / o corpo de jurados

9. evidence
a evidência / as provas

10. prosecuting attorney
o promotor

11. witness
a testemunha

12. court reporter
o escrevente

13. bailiff
o oficial de justiça / o meirinho

"Guilty."

"7 years."

E. give the verdict*
dar o veredicto

F. sentence the defendant
sentenciar o réu

G. go to jail / **go** to prison
ir para a prisão

14. convict
o condenado / o preso

H. be released
ser solto

*Note: There are two possible verdicts, "guilty" and "not guilty."

Share your answers.

1. What are some differences between the legal system in the United States and the one in your country?

2. Do you want to be on a jury? Why or why not?

1. **vandalism**
   o vandalismo

2. **gang violence**
   a violência de gangue

3. **drunk driving**
   dirigir embriagado

4. **illegal drugs**
   as drogas ilegais

5. **mugging**
   o assalto

6. **burglary**
   o roubo

7. **assault**
   o ataque

8. **murder**
   o assassinato

9. **gun**
   o revólver

More vocabulary

commit a crime: to do something illegal

criminal: someone who commits a crime

victim: someone who is hurt or killed by someone else

Share your answers.

1. Is there too much crime on TV? in the movies?

2. Do you think people become criminals from watching crime on TV?

A. **Walk** with a friend.
Ande com um amigo.

B. **Stay** on well-lit streets.
Permaneça em ruas bem iluminadas.

C. **Hold** your purse close to your body.
Segure sua bolsa próxima ao seu corpo.

D. **Protect** your wallet.
Proteja sua carteira.

E. **Lock** your doors.
Tranque as portas.

F. **Don't open** your door to strangers.
Não abra a porta para estranhos.

G. **Don't drink** and **drive**.
Não dirija depois de beber.

H. **Report** crimes to the police.
Comunique crimes à polícia.

More vocabulary

Neighborhood Watch: a group of neighbors who watch for criminals in their neighborhood

designated drivers: people who don't drink alcoholic beverages so that they can drive drinkers home

Share your answers.

1. Do you feel safe in your neighborhood?

2. Look at the pictures. Which of these things do you do?

3. What other things do you do to stay safe?

1. **lost child**
   a criança perdida

2. **car accident**
   o acidente de automóvel

3. **airplane crash**
   o acidente de avião

4. **explosion**
   a explosão

5. **earthquake**
   o terremoto

6. **mudslide**
   o deslizamento de terra

7. **fire**
   o incêndio

8. **firefighter**
   o bombeiro

9. **fire truck**
   o caminhão de bombeiro

Practice reporting a fire.

This is <u>Lisa Broad</u>. There is a fire.

The address is <u>323 Oak Street.</u>

Please send someone quickly.

Share your answers.

1. Can you give directions to your home if there is a fire?

2. What information do you give to the other driver if you are in a car accident?

10. drought
a seca

11. blizzard
a tempestade de neve / a nevasca

12. hurricane
o furacão

13. tornado
o ciclone

14. volcanic eruption
a erupção vulcânica

15. tidal wave
o maremoto

16. flood
a inundação

17. search and rescue team
a equipe de resgate

Share your answers.

1. Which disasters are common in your area? Which never happen?

2. What can you do to prepare for emergencies?

3. Do you have emergency numbers near your telephone?

4. What organizations will help you in an emergency?

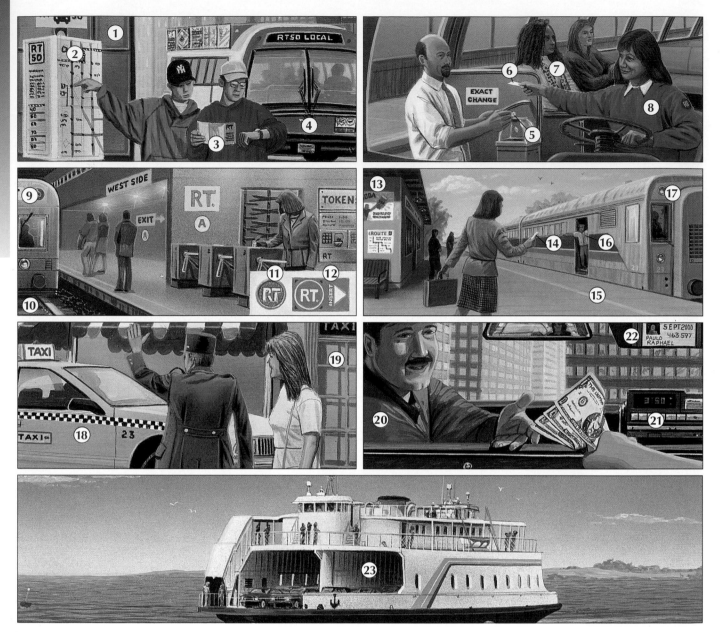

1. **bus stop**
   o ponto de ônibus

2. **route**
   a rota

3. **schedule**
   o horário

4. **bus**
   o ônibus

5. **fare**
   a passagem

6. **transfer**
   o bilhete de integração

7. **passenger**
   a passageira

8. **bus driver**
   a motorista de ônibus

9. **subway**
   o metrô

10. **track**
    os trilhos

11. **token**
    a ficha de metrô

12. **fare card**
    a passagem / o bilhete de metrô

13. **train station**
    a estação de trem

14. **ticket**
    o bilhete

15. **platform**
    a plataforma

16. **conductor**
    o chefe de trem

17. **train**
    o trem

18. **taxi / cab**
    o táxi

19. **taxi stand**
    o ponto de táxi

20. **taxi driver**
    o motorista de táxi

21. **meter**
    o taxímetro

22. **taxi license**
    a licença de táxi

23. **ferry**
    a balsa

More vocabulary

hail a taxi: to get a taxi driver's attention by raising your hand

miss the bus: to arrive at the bus stop late

Talk about how you and your friends come to school.

I take _the bus_ to school.   He _drives_ to school.
You take _the train_.   She _walks_ to school.
We take _the subway_.   They _ride_ bikes.

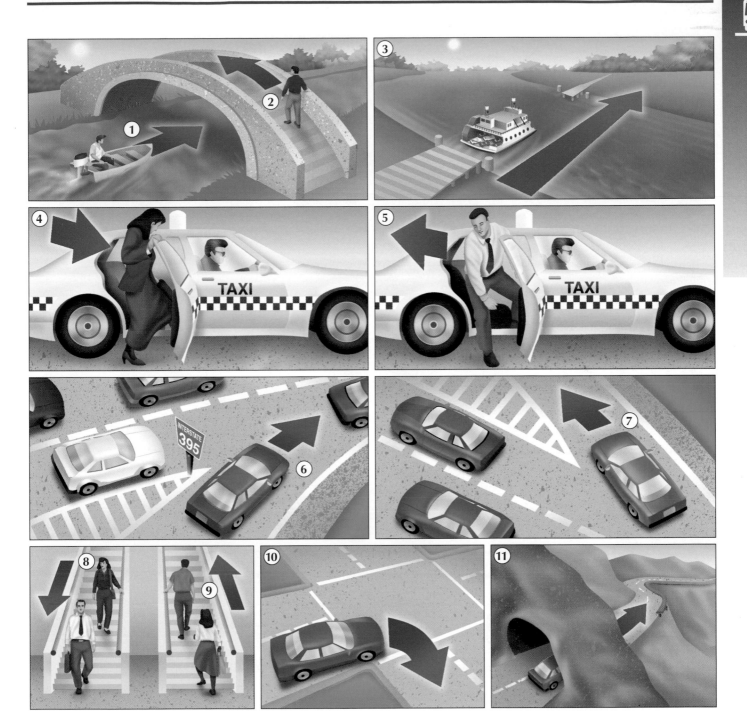

1. **under** the bridge
   por baixo da ponte / sob a ponte

2. **over** the bridge
   por cima da ponte / sobre a ponte

3. **across** the water
   para o outro lado do rio

4. **into** the taxi
   para dentro do táxi

5. **out of** the taxi
   para fora do táxi

6. **onto** the highway
   entrar na estrada

7. **off** the highway
   sair da estrada

8. **down** the stairs
   escada abaixo / descer a escada

9. **up** the stairs
   escada acima / subir a escada

10. **around** the corner
    dobrar a esquina / virar a esquina

11. **through** the tunnel
    através do túnel / pelo túnel

Grammar point: *into, out of, on, off*

We say, *get **into** a taxi or a car.*

But we say, *get **on** a bus, a train, or a plane.*

We say, *get **out of** a taxi or a car.*

But we say, *get **off** a bus, a train, or a plane.*

1. **subcompact**
   o subcompacto

2. **compact**
   o compacto

3. **midsize car**
   o carro médio

4. **full-size car**
   o carro grande

5. **convertible**
   o conversível

6. **sports car**
   o carro-esporte

7. **pickup truck**
   a picape / a caminhonete

8. **station wagon**
   a perua

9. **SUV (sports utility vehicle)**
   o utilitário esportivo

10. **minivan**
    a minivan

11. **camper**
    o trailer / o motorhome

12. **dump truck**
    o caminhão basculante

13. **tow truck**
    o guincho

14. **moving van**
    o caminhão de mudança

15. **tractor trailer / semi**
    a carreta / o caminhão semi-reboque

16. **cab**
    a cabine

17. **trailer**
    o semi-reboque / a carreta-baú

More vocabulary

make: the name of the company that makes the car

model: the style of car

Share your answers.

1. What is your favorite kind of car?

2. What kind of car is good for a big family? for a single person?

Directions   Direções

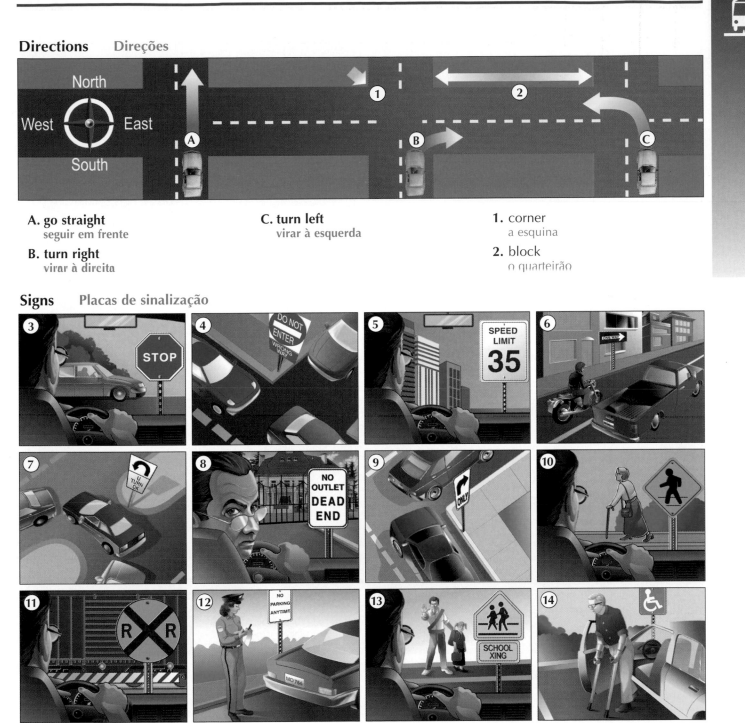

A. go straight
seguir em frente

B. turn right
virar à direita

C. turn left
virar à esquerda

1. corner
a esquina

2. block
o quarteirão

Signs   Placas de sinalização

3. stop
pare / parada obrigatória

4. do not enter/wrong way
contramão / sentido proibido

5. speed limit
velocidade máxima permitida

6. one way
mão única / sentido obrigatório

7. U-turn OK
retorno permitido

8. no outlet/dead end
rua sem saída

9. right turn only
virar (somente) à direita

10. pedestrian crossing
travessia de pedestre / passagem
de pedestre

11. railroad crossing
cruzamento ferroviário / passagem
de nível

12. no parking
proibido estacionar

13. school crossing
travessia escolar / área escolar

14. handicapped parking
estacionamento para deficientes

More vocabulary

right-of-way: the right to go first

yield: to give another person or car the right-of-way

Share your answers.

1. Which traffic signs are the same in your country?

2. Do pedestrians have the right-of-way in your city?

3. What is the speed limit in front of your school?
your home?

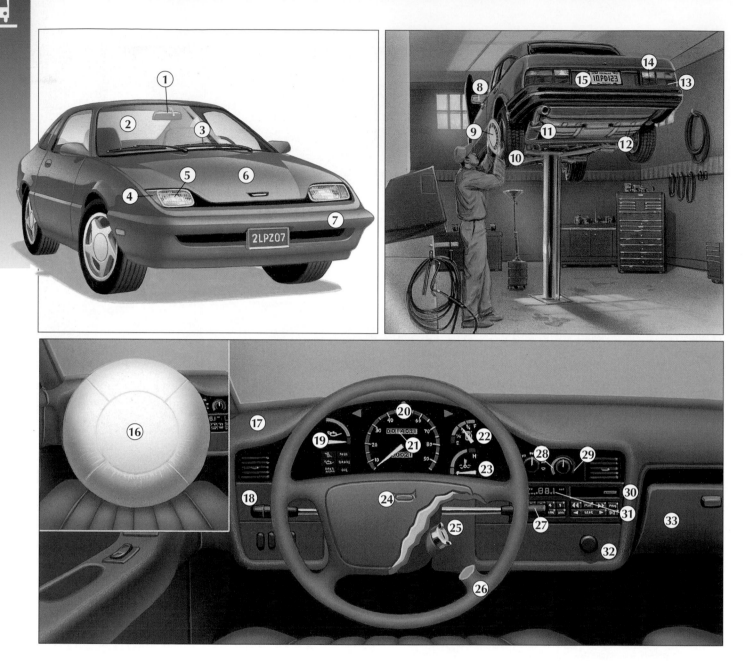

1. rearview mirror
   o espelho retrovisor

2. windshield
   o pára-brisa

3. windshield wipers
   os limpadores de
   pára-brisa

4. turn signal
   o pisca-pisca

5. headlight
   o farol dianteiro

6. hood
   o capô

7. bumper
   o pára-choque

8. sideview mirror
   o espelho retrovisor
   externo

9. hubcap
   a calota

10. tire
    o pneu

11. muffler
    o silencioso

12. gas tank
    o tanque de gasolina

13. brake light
    a luz de freio

14. taillight
    a lanterna traseira

15. license plate
    a placa

16. air bag
    o air bag

17. dashboard
    o painel

18. turn signal
    o pisca-pisca / a alavanca
    dos sinalizadores

19. oil gauge
    o indicador do óleo

20. speedometer
    o velocímetro

21. odometer
    o hodômetro

22. gas gauge
    o indicador de gasolina

23. temperature gauge
    o indicador de
    temperatura

24. horn
    a buzina

25. ignition
    a ignição

26. steering wheel
    o volante

27. gearshift
    a alavanca do câmbio

28. air conditioning
    o ar-condicionado

29. heater
    o aquecedor

30. tape deck
    o toca-fitas

31. radio
    o rádio

32. cigarette lighter
    o acendedor de cigarro

33. glove compartment
    o porta-luvas

34. lock
a trava

35. front seat
o banco dianteiro

36. seat belt
o cinto de segurança (subabdominal)

37. shoulder harness
o cinto de segurança (transversal)

38. backseat
o banco traseiro

39. child safety seat
o assento para criança / a cadeira
para auto

40. fuel injection system
o sistema de injeção de combustível

41. engine
o motor

42. radiator
o radiador

43. battery
a bateria

44. emergency brake
o freio de estacionamento

45. clutch*
o pedal da embreagem

46. brake pedal
o pedal do freio

47. accelerator / gas pedal
o pedal do acelerador

48. stick shift
(a alavanca d)o câmbio

49. trunk
o porta-malas

50. lug wrench
a chave-de-rodas

51. jack
o macaco

52. jumper cables
os cabos para passar corrente

53. spare tire
o estepe

54. The car needs **gas**.
O carro precisa de **combustível**.

55. The car needs **oil**.
O carro precisa de **óleo**.

56. The radiator needs **coolant**.
O radiador precisa de **fluido (para
radiador)**.

57. The car needs **a smog check**.
O carro precisa de uma **regulagem /
checagem** de emissão de gases.

58. The battery needs **recharging**.
A bateria precisa ser **recarregada**.

59. The tires need **air**.
É preciso **encher** os pneus.

*Note: Standard transmission cars have a
clutch; automatic transmission cars do not.

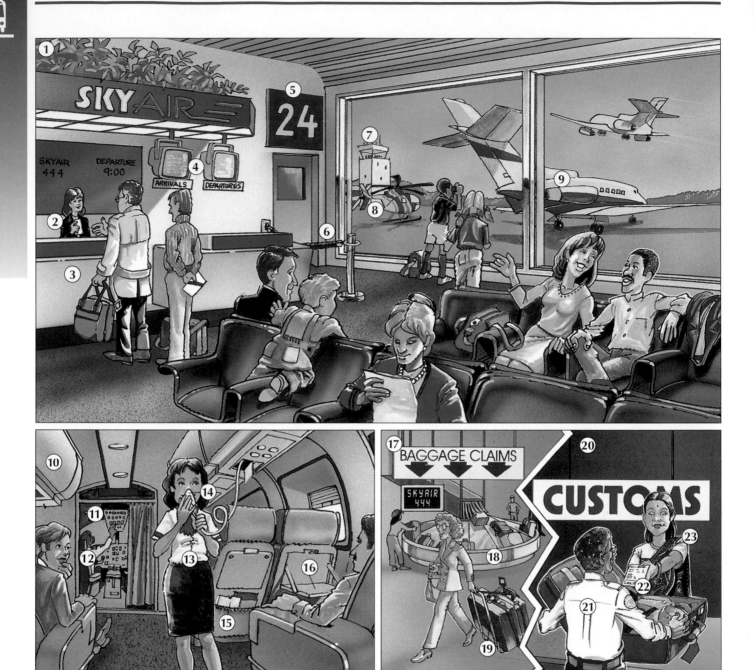

1. **airline terminal**
   o balcão da empresa aérea

2. **airline representative**
   a atendente da empresa aérea

3. **check-in counter**
   o balcão de embarque

4. **arrival and departure monitors**
   os monitores de chegada e partida

5. **gate**
   o portão de embarque

6. **boarding area**
   a área de embarque

7. **control tower**
   a torre de controle

8. **helicopter**
   o helicóptero

9. **airplane**
   o avião

10. **overhead compartment**
    o compartimento para bagagem
    de mão

11. **cockpit**
    a cabine do piloto / a cabine
    de comando

12. **pilot**
    o piloto / o comandante

13. **flight attendant**
    a aeromoça / a comissária de bordo

14. **oxygen mask**
    a máscara de oxigênio

15. **airsickness bag**
    os sacos para enjôo

16. **tray table**
    a mesinha individual

17. **baggage claim area**
    o terminal de bagagem

18. **carousel**
    a esteira

19. **luggage carrier**
    o carrinho de bagagem

20. **customs**
    a alfândega

21. **customs officer**
    o agente da alfândega

22. **declaration form**
    o formulário de declaração para
    a alfândega

23. **passenger**
    a passageira

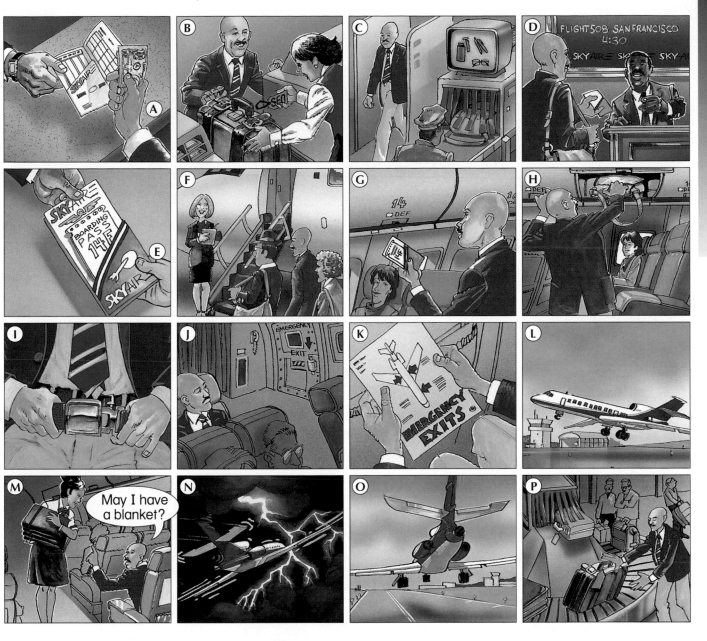

A. **buy** your ticket
comprar a passagem

B. **check** your bags
despachar a bagagem

C. **go through** security
passar pela segurança

D. **check in** at the gate
apresentar-se no portão

E. **get** your boarding pass
pegar o cartão de embarque

F. **board** the plane
embarcar no avião

G. **find** your seat
encontrar a poltrona

H. **stow** your carry-on bag
guardar a bagagem de mão

I. **fasten** your seat belt
colocar / ajustar o cinto de segurança

J. **look for** the emergency exit
procurar / localizar a saída de emergência

K. **look at** the emergency card
olhar a ficha de emergência

L. **take off / leave**
decolar / partir

M. **request** a blanket
pedir um cobertor

N. **experience** turbulence
passar por turbulência

O. **land / arrive**
aterrissar / chegar

P. **claim** your baggage
pegar / retirar a bagagem

More vocabulary

destination: the place the passenger is going

departure time: the time the plane takes off

arrival time: the time the plane lands

direct flight: a plane trip between two cities with no stops

stopover: a stop before reaching the destination, sometimes to change planes

1. public school
a escola pública

2. private school
a escola particular

3. parochial school
a escola religiosa

4. preschool
a pré-escola

5. elementary school
a 1a. – 4a. séries do
Ensino Fundamental

6. middle school /
junior high school
a 5a. – 8a. séries do
Ensino Fundamental

7. high school
Ensino Médio

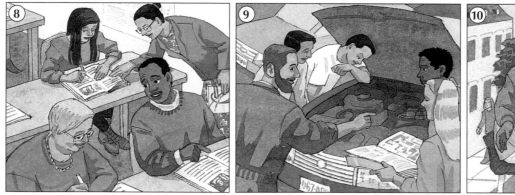

8. adult school
a escola para adultos

9. vocational school / trade school
a escola técnica

10. college / university
a faculdade / a universidade

Note: In the U.S. most children begin school at age 5 (in kindergarten)
and graduate from high school at 17 or 18.

More vocabulary

When students graduate from a college or university
they receive a **degree**:

Bachelor's degree— usually 4 years of study

Master's degree—an additional 1–3 years of study

Doctorate—an additional 3–5 years of study

community college: a two-year college where students
can get an Associate of Arts degree

graduate school: a school in a university where students
study for their master's and doctorates

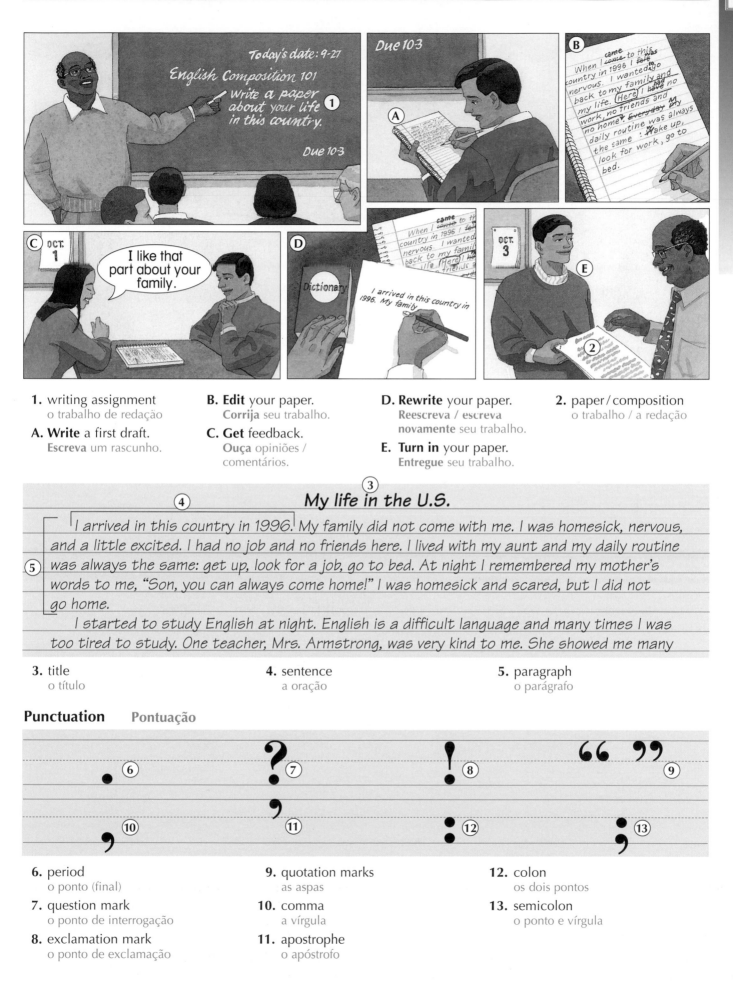

1. writing assignment
o trabalho de redação

A. Write a first draft.
Escreva um rascunho.

B. Edit your paper.
Corrija seu trabalho.

C. Get feedback.
Ouça opiniões / comentários.

D. Rewrite your paper.
Reescreva / escreva novamente seu trabalho.

E. Turn in your paper.
Entregue seu trabalho.

2. paper / composition
o trabalho / a redação

My life in the U.S.

I arrived in this country in 1996. My family did not come with me. I was homesick, nervous, and a little excited. I had no job and no friends here. I lived with my aunt and my daily routine was always the same: get up, look for a job, go to bed. At night I remembered my mother's words to me, "Son, you can always come home!" I was homesick and scared, but I did not go home.

I started to study English at night. English is a difficult language and many times I was too tired to study. One teacher, Mrs. Armstrong, was very kind to me. She showed me many

3. title
o título

4. sentence
a oração

5. paragraph
o parágrafo

Punctuation   Pontuação

6. period
o ponto (final)

7. question mark
o ponto de interrogação

8. exclamation mark
o ponto de exclamação

9. quotation marks
as aspas

10. comma
a vírgula

11. apostrophe
o apóstrofo

12. colon
os dois pontos

13. semicolon
o ponto e vírgula

Exploration

War

Immigration

| **Historical and Political Events**
Acontecimentos históricos e políticos | **1492 →**
French, Spanish, English explorers
exploradores franceses, espanhóis e ingleses | **1607–1750**
Colonies along Atlantic coast founded by Northern Europeans
colônias ao longo da costa do Atlântico fundadas por imigrantes do norte da Europa | **1619** 1st African slave sold in Virginia
primeira venda de um escravo africano na Virgínia

1653 1st Indian reservation in Virginia
primeira reserva indígena na Virgínia |

Before 1700   **1700**

| **Immigration***
Imigração | **1607**
1st English in Virginia
primeiro inglês na Virgínia | **1610**
Spanish at Santa Fe
espanhóis em Santa Fé | |

| **Population****
População | Before 1700: Native American: 1,000,000+
nativos americanos 1.000.000+ | | 1700: colonists: 250,000
colonos 250.000 |

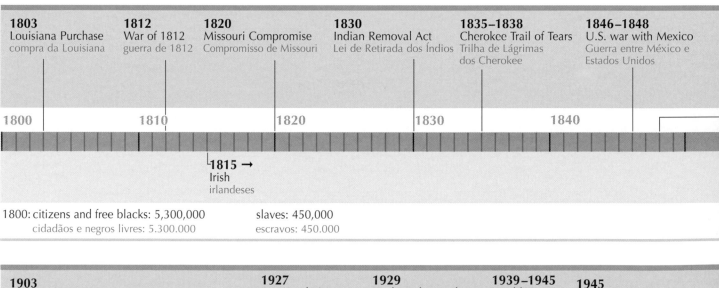

| **1803**
Louisiana Purchase
compra da Louisiana | **1812**
War of 1812
guerra de 1812 | **1820**
Missouri Compromise
Compromisso de Missouri | **1830**
Indian Removal Act
Lei de Retirada dos Índios | **1835–1838**
Cherokee Trail of Tears
Trilha de Lágrimas dos Cherokee | **1846–1848**
U.S. war with Mexico
Guerra entre México e Estados Unidos |

1800   **1810**   **1820**   **1830**   **1840**

1815 →
Irish
irlandeses

1800: citizens and free blacks: 5,300,000   slaves: 450,000
cidadãos e negros livres: 5.300.000   escravos: 450.000

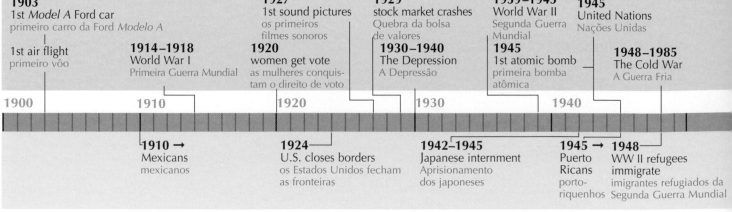

| **1903**
1st *Model A* Ford car
primeiro carro da Ford *Modelo A*

1st air flight
primeiro vôo | **1914–1918**
World War I
Primeira Guerra Mundial | **1927**
1st sound pictures
os primeiros filmes sonoros

1920
women get vote
as mulheres conquistam o direito de voto | **1929**
stock market crashes
Quebra da bolsa de valores

1930–1940
The Depression
A Depressão | **1939–1945**
World War II
Segunda Guerra Mundial

1945
1st atomic bomb
primeira bomba atômica | **1945**
United Nations
Nações Unidas

1948–1985
The Cold War
A Guerra Fria |

1900   **1910**   **1920**   **1930**   **1940**

1910 →
Mexicans
mexicanos

1924
U.S. closes borders
os Estados Unidos fecham as fronteiras

1942–1945
Japanese internment
Aprisionamento dos japoneses

1945 →
Puerto Ricans
portoriquenhos

1948
WW II refugees immigrate
imigrantes refugiados da Segunda Guerra Mundial

1900: 75,994,000

*Immigration dates indicate a time when large numbers of that group first began to immigrate to the U.S.
**All population figures before 1790 are estimates. Figures after 1790 are based on the official U.S. census.

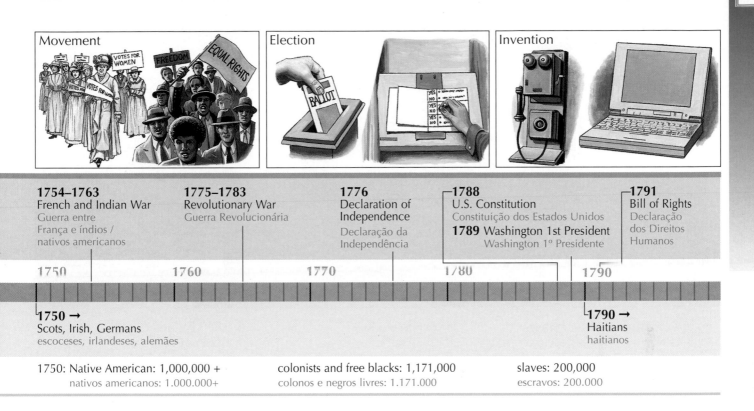

Movement

Election

Invention

1754–1763
French and Indian War
Guerra entre
França e índios /
nativos americanos

1775–1783
Revolutionary War
Guerra Revolucionária

1776
Declaration of
Independence
Declaração da
Independência

1788
U.S. Constitution
Constituição dos Estados Unidos
1789 Washington 1st President
Washington 1° Presidente

1791
Bill of Rights
Declaração
dos Direitos
Humanos

1750   1760   1770   1780   1790

1750 →
Scots, Irish, Germans
escoceses, irlandeses, alemães

1790 →
Haitians
haitianos

1750: Native American: 1,000,000 +
nativos americanos: 1.000.000+

colonists and free blacks: 1,171,000
colonos e negros livres: 1.171.000

slaves: 200,000
escravos: 200.000

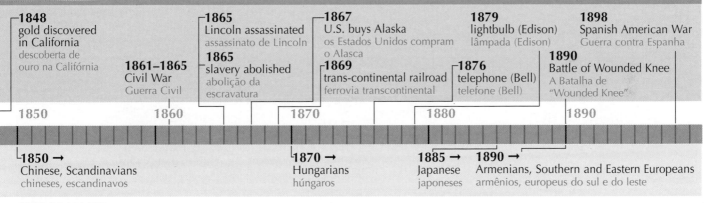

1848
gold discovered
in California
descoberta de
ouro na Califórnia

1865
Lincoln assassinated
assassinato de Lincoln
1865
slavery abolished
abolição da
escravatura

1867
U.S. buys Alaska
os Estados Unidos compram
o Alasca
1869
trans-continental railroad
ferrovia transcontinental

1879
lightbulb (Edison)
lâmpada (Edison)

1876
telephone (Bell)
telefone (Bell)

1898
Spanish American War
Guerra contra Espanha
1890
Battle of Wounded Knee
A Batalha de
"Wounded Knee"

1861–1865
Civil War
Guerra Civil

1850   1860   1870   1880   1890

1850 →
Chinese, Scandinavians
chineses, escandinavos

1870 →
Hungarians
húngaros

1885 →
Japanese
japoneses

1890 →
Armenians, Southern and Eastern Europeans
armênios, europeus do sul e do leste

1850: 23,191,000

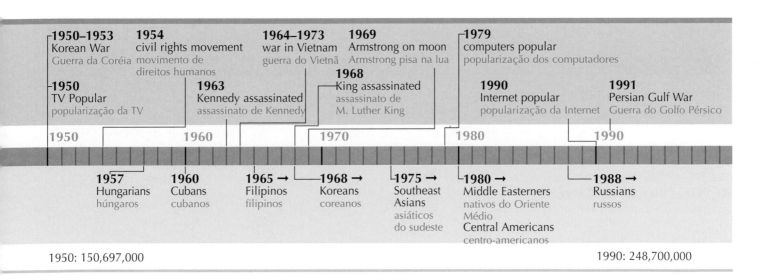

1950–1953
Korean War
Guerra da Coréia
1950
TV Popular
popularização da TV

1954
civil rights movement
movimento de
direitos humanos

1964–1973
war in Vietnam
guerra do Vietnã

1963
Kennedy assassinated
assassinato de Kennedy

1969
Armstrong on moon
Armstrong pisa na lua
1968
King assassinated
assassinato de
M. Luther King

1979
computers popular
popularização dos computadores

1990
Internet popular
popularização da Internet

1991
Persian Gulf War
Guerra do Golfo Pérsico

1950   1960   1970   1980   1990

1957
Hungarians
húngaros

1960
Cubans
cubanos

1965 →
Filipinos
filipinos

1968 →
Koreans
coreanos

1975 →
Southeast
Asians
asiáticos
do sudeste

1980 →
Middle Easterners
nativos do Oriente
Médio
Central Americans
centro-americanos

1988 →
Russians
russos

1950: 150,697,000

1990: 248,700,000

BRANCHES OF GOVERNMENT

Legislative | Executive | Judicial

1. **The House of Representatives**
   A Câmara dos Deputados

2. **congresswoman / congressman**
   a deputada / a congressista

3. **The Senate**
   O Senado

4. **senator**
   o senador

5. **The White House**
   A Casa Branca

6. **president**
   o presidente

7. **vice president**
   o vice-presidente

8. **The Supreme Court**
   O Tribunal Superior /
   A Suprema Corte

9. **chief justice**
   o presidente do tribunal superior

10. **justices**
    os juízes

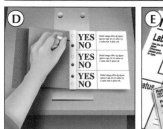

Citizenship application requirements
Requisitos para solicitação de cidadania

A. **be** 18 years old
   ter 18 anos completos

B. **live** in the U.S. for five years
   morar nos Estados Unidos por cinco anos

C. **take** a citizenship test
   fazer um teste de cidadania

Rights and responsibilities
Direitos e responsabilidades

D. **vote**
   votar

E. **pay** taxes
   pagar impostos

F. **register** with Selective Service*
   alistar-se para o Serviço Militar

G. **serve** on a jury
   servir como jurado

H. **obey** the law
   cumprir a lei

*Note: All males 18 to 26 who live in the U.S. are required to register with Selective Service.

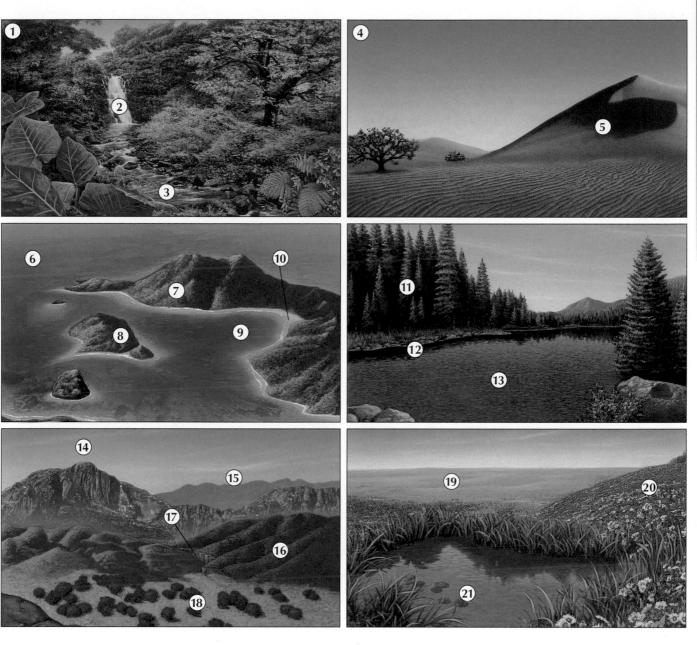

1. **rain forest**
   a floresta tropical / equatorial

2. **waterfall**
   a cachoeira

3. **river**
   o rio

4. **desert**
   o deserto

5. **sand dune**
   as dunas de areia

6. **ocean**
   o oceano

7. **peninsula**
   a península

8. **island**
   a ilha

9. **bay**
   a baía

10. **beach**
    a praia

11. **forest**
    a floresta

12. **shore**
    a margem

13. **lake**
    o lago

14. **mountain peak**
    o pico / o topo da montanha

15. **mountain range**
    a cordilheira / a serra

16. **hills**
    as colinas

17. **canyon**
    o desfiladeiro

18. **valley**
    o vale

19. **plains**
    a planície

20. **meadow**
    a campina

21. **pond**
    o pequeno lago

More vocabulary

a body of water: a river, lake, or ocean

stream/creek: a very small river

Talk about where you live and where you like to go.

I live in a valley. There is a lake nearby.

I like to go to the beach.

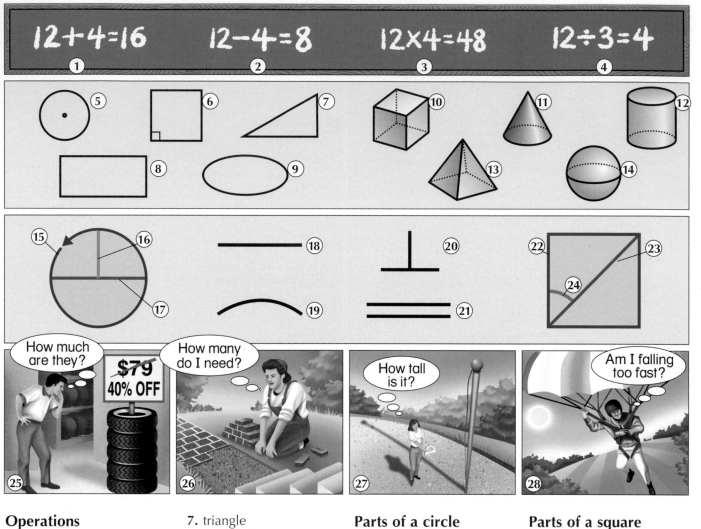

Operations
Operações matemáticas

1. addition
   a adição

2. subtraction
   a subtração

3. multiplication
   a multiplicação

4. division
   a divisão

Shapes
Figuras geométricas

5. circle
   o círculo

6. square
   o quadrado

7. triangle
   o triângulo

8. rectangle
   o retângulo

9. oval / ellipse
   o oval / a elipse

Solids
Sólidos

10. cube
    o cubo

11. cone
    o cone

12. cylinder
    o cilindro

13. pyramid
    a pirâmide

14. sphere
    a esfera

Parts of a circle
Partes de um círculo

15. circumference
    a circunferência

16. radius
    o raio

17. diameter
    o diâmetro

Lines
Linhas

18. straight
    reta

19. curved
    curva

20. perpendicular
    perpendicular

21. parallel
    paralela

Parts of a square
Partes de um quadrado

22. side
    o lado

23. diagonal
    a diagonal

24. angle
    o ângulo

Types of math
Tipos de matemática

25. algebra
    a álgebra

26. geometry
    a geometria

27. trigonometry
    a trigonometria

28. calculus
    o cálculo

More vocabulary

total: the answer to an addition problem

difference: the answer to a subtraction problem

product: the answer to a multiplication problem

quotient: the answer to a division problem

pi (π): the number when you divide the circumference of a circle by its diameter (approximately = 3.14)

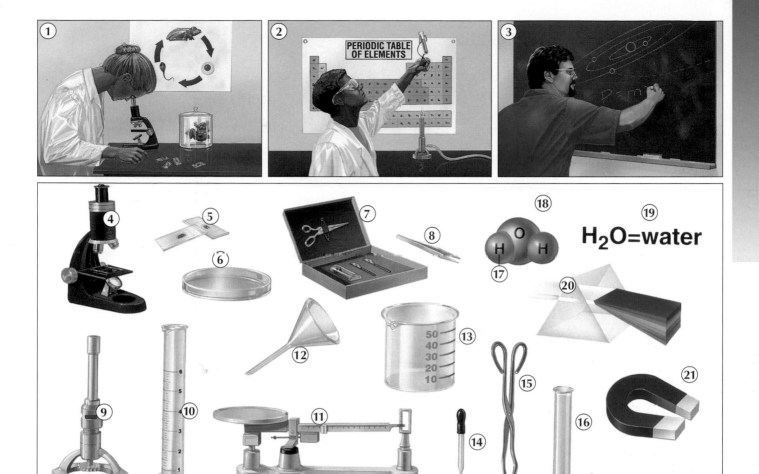

H_2O=water

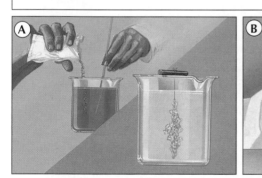

1. biology
   a biologia

2. chemistry
   a química

3. physics
   a física

4. microscope
   o microscópio

5. slide
   a lâmina

6. petri dish
   a placa de Petri

7. dissection kit
   o kit / o estojo de dissecação

8. forceps
   a pinça

9. Bunsen burner
   o bico de Bunsen

10. graduated cylinder
    a proveta graduada

11. balance
    a balança

12. funnel
    o funil

13. beaker
    o béquer

14. dropper
    o conta-gotas

15. crucible tongs
    o torquês de cadinho / a pinça de cadinho

16. test tube
    o tubo de ensaio

17. atom
    o átomo

18. molecule
    a molécula

19. formula
    a fórmula

20. prism
    o prisma

21. magnet
    o ímã

A. **do** an experiment
   fazer uma experiência

B. **observe**
   observar

C. **record** results
   anotar os resultados

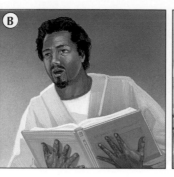

A. **play** an instrument
tocar um instrumento

B. **sing** a song
cantar uma canção

1. orchestra
a orquestra

2. rock band
o conjunto de rock /
a banda de rock

Woodwinds

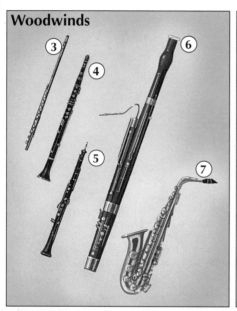

Strings

Brass

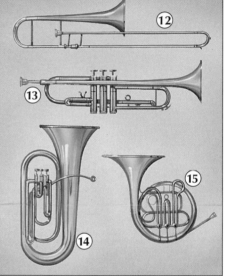

Percussion

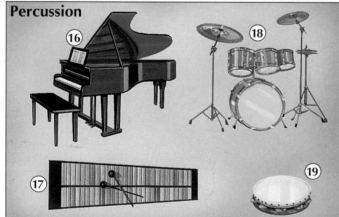

Other Instruments

3. flute
a flauta

4. clarinet
o clarinete

5. oboe
o oboé

6. bassoon
o fagote

7. saxophone
o saxofone

8. violin
o violino

9. cello
o violoncelo

10. bass
o (contra) baixo

11. guitar
o violão

12. trombone
o trombone

13. trumpet / horn
o trompete

14. tuba
a tuba

15. French horn
a trompa

16. piano
o piano

17. xylophone
o xilofone

18. drums
a bateria

19. tambourine
o pandeiro

20. electric keyboard
o teclado elétrico

21. accordion
o acordeão

22. organ
o órgão

1. art
   educação artística

2. business education
   educação comercial

3. chorus
   coral

4. computer science
   informática / computação

5. driver's education
   aulas de direção

6. economics
   economia

7. English as a second language
   inglês (como segunda língua)

8. foreign language
   língua estrangeira

9. home economics
   economia doméstica

10. industrial arts / shop
    artes industriais / oficina

11. PE (physical education)
    educação física

12. theater arts
    arte dramática

More vocabulary

core course: a subject students have to take

elective: a subject students choose to take

Share your answers.

1. What are your favorite subjects?

2. In your opinion, what subjects are most important? Why?

3. What foreign languages are taught in your school?

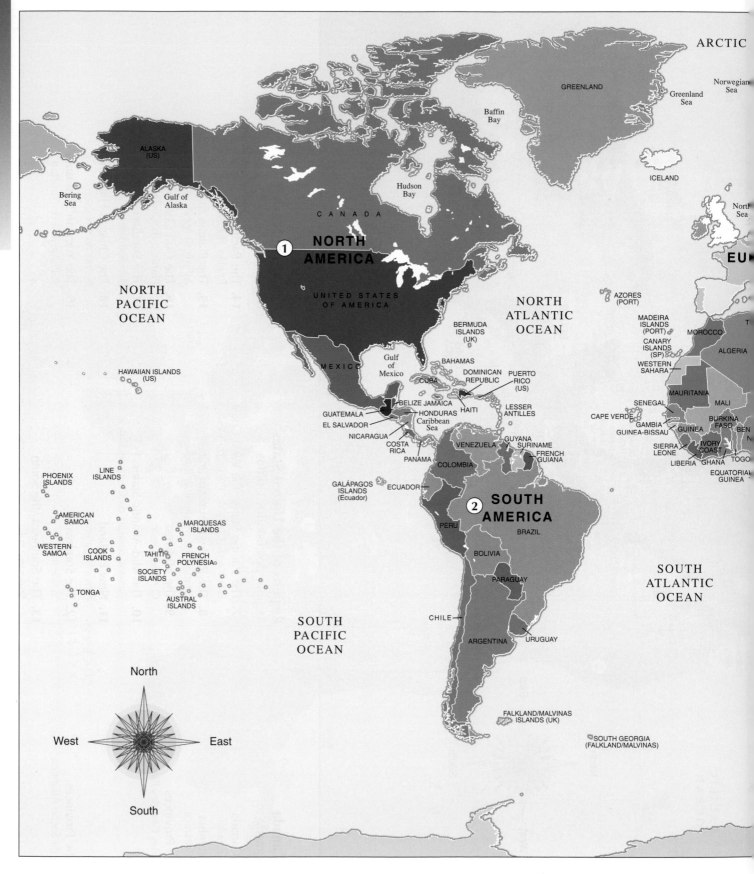

ARCTIC

GREENLAND

Norwegian
Sea

Greenland
Sea

Baffin
Bay

ICELAND

Bering
Sea

Gulf of
Alaska

ALASKA
(US)

Hudson
Bay

North
Sea

CANADA

NORTH
PACIFIC
OCEAN

① NORTH
AMERICA

UNITED STATES
OF AMERICA

EU

NORTH
ATLANTIC
OCEAN

AZORES
(PORT)

MADEIRA
ISLANDS
(PORT)

MOROCCO

CANARY
ISLANDS
(SP)

ALGERIA

WESTERN
SAHARA

BERMUDA
ISLANDS
(UK)

MEXICO

Gulf
of
Mexico

BAHAMAS

CUBA

DOMINICAN
REPUBLIC

PUERTO
RICO
(US)

MAURITANIA

MALI

HAWAIIAN ISLANDS
(US)

BELIZE JAMAICA

GUATEMALA

EL SALVADOR

HONDURAS

HAITI

LESSER
ANTILLES

CAPE VERDE

SENEGAL

GAMBIA

GUINEA-BISSAU

BURKINA
FASO

BEN

Caribbean
Sea

NICARAGUA

COSTA
RICA

PANAMA

VENEZUELA

GUYANA

SURINAME

FRENCH
GUIANA

SIERRA
LEONE

GUINEA

IVORY
COAST

TOGO

LIBERIA

GHANA

PHOENIX
ISLANDS

LINE
ISLANDS

COLOMBIA

EQUATORIAL
GUINEA

GALÁPAGOS
ISLANDS
(Ecuador)

ECUADOR

AMERICAN
SAMOA

MARQUESAS
ISLANDS

② SOUTH
AMERICA

PERU

BRAZIL

WESTERN
SAMOA

COOK
ISLANDS

TAHITI

FRENCH
POLYNESIA

BOLIVIA

SOUTH
ATLANTIC
OCEAN

SOCIETY
ISLANDS

PARAGUAY

TONGA

AUSTRAL
ISLANDS

SOUTH
PACIFIC
OCEAN

CHILE

ARGENTINA

URUGUAY

North

West

East

South

FALKLAND/MALVINAS
ISLANDS (UK)

SOUTH GEORGIA
(FALKLAND/MALVINAS)

Continents
Continentes

1. North America
América do Norte

2. South America
América do Sul

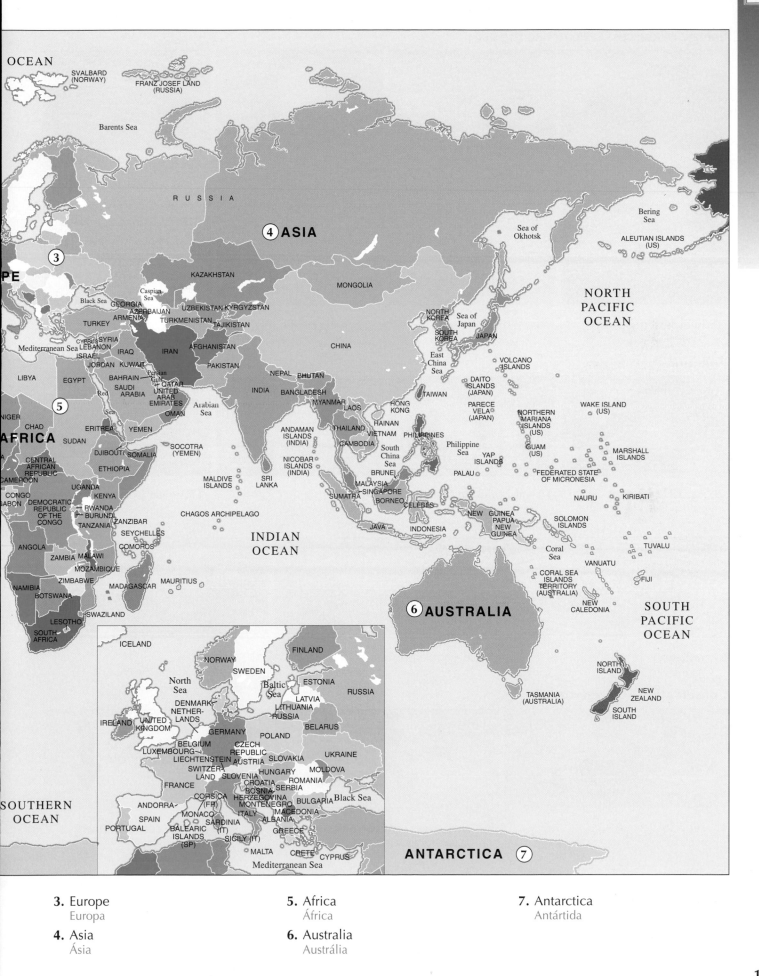

OCEAN

SVALBARD (NORWAY)

FRANZ JOSEF LAND (RUSSIA)

Barents Sea

R U S S I A

③

④ ASIA

KAZAKHSTAN

MONGOLIA

Sea of Okhotsk

Bering Sea

ALEUTIAN ISLANDS (US)

Caspian Sea

Black Sea GEORGIA
AZERBAIJAN
ARMENIA
TURKEY
UZBEKISTAN KYRGYZSTAN
TURKMENISTAN TAJIKISTAN

NORTH KOREA
Sea of Japan
SOUTH KOREA
JAPAN

NORTH PACIFIC OCEAN

Mediterranean Sea
CYPRUS SYRIA
LEBANON
ISRAEL
IRAQ
JORDAN KUWAIT
AFGHANISTAN
IRAN
PAKISTAN
CHINA
East China Sea

LIBYA
EGYPT
BAHRAIN
SAUDI ARABIA
QATAR
UNITED ARAB EMIRATES
OMAN
Persian Gulf
Red Sea
Arabian Sea
⑤
NEPAL BHUTAN
INDIA
BANGLADESH
MYANMAR
LAOS
TAIWAN
HONG KONG

VOLCANO ISLANDS

DAITO ISLANDS (JAPAN)

PARECE VELA (JAPAN)

WAKE ISLAND (US)

NIGER
CHAD
AFRICA
SUDAN
ERITREA YEMEN
SOCOTRA (YEMEN)
THAILAND
HAINAN
VIETNAM
PHILIPPINES
NORTHERN MARIANA ISLANDS (US)
GUAM (US)
MARSHALL ISLANDS

CENTRAL AFRICAN REPUBLIC
CAMEROON
DJIBOUTI SOMALIA
ETHIOPIA
CAMBODIA
ANDAMAN ISLANDS (INDIA)
NICOBAR ISLANDS (INDIA)
South China Sea
Philippine Sea
YAP ISLANDS
PALAU
FEDERATED STATE OF MICRONESIA

CONGO
GABON
UGANDA
KENYA
MALDIVE ISLANDS
SRI LANKA
BRUNEI
MALAYSIA
SINGAPORE
BORNEO
NAURU
KIRIBATI

DEMOCRATIC REPUBLIC OF THE CONGO
RWANDA
BURUNDI
TANZANIA ZANZIBAR
SEYCHELLES
CHAGOS ARCHIPELAGO
SUMATRA
CELEBES
JAVA INDONESIA
NEW GUINEA
PAPUA NEW GUINEA
SOLOMON ISLANDS
TUVALU

ANGOLA
ZAMBIA MALAWI
MOZAMBIQUE
INDIAN OCEAN
Coral Sea
VANUATU

NAMIBIA
ZIMBABWE
BOTSWANA
MADAGASCAR
MAURITIUS
CORAL SEA ISLANDS TERRITORY (AUSTRALIA)
FIJI

LESOTHO
SWAZILAND
⑥ AUSTRALIA
NEW CALEDONIA
SOUTH PACIFIC OCEAN

SOUTH AFRICA

ICELAND
FINLAND
NORWAY
SWEDEN
North Sea
Baltic Sea
ESTONIA
RUSSIA
LATVIA
LITHUANIA
RUSSIA
DENMARK
NETHER-LANDS
IRELAND
UNITED KINGDOM
GERMANY
POLAND
BELARUS
BELGIUM
LUXEMBOURG
LIECHTENSTEIN
CZECH REPUBLIC
AUSTRIA SLOVAKIA
UKRAINE
SWITZER-LAND
SLOVENIA
HUNGARY
MOLDOVA
FRANCE
CROATIA
ROMANIA
CORSICA (FR)
BOSNIA HERZEGOVINA
SERBIA
ANDORRA
MONACO
MONTENEGRO
BULGARIA Black Sea
SPAIN
ITALY
MACEDONIA
SARDINIA (IT)
ALBANIA
PORTUGAL
BALEARIC ISLANDS (SP)
SICILY (IT)
GREECE
MALTA
CRETE
CYPRUS
Mediterranean Sea

NORTH ISLAND
TASMANIA (AUSTRALIA)
NEW ZEALAND
SOUTH ISLAND

SOUTHERN OCEAN

ANTARCTICA ⑦

3. Europe
Europa

4. Asia
Ásia

5. Africa
África

6. Australia
Austrália

7. Antarctica
Antártida

Energy and the Environment   Energia e meio ambiente

Energy resources   Fontes de energia

1. solar energy
a energia solar

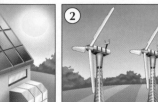

2. wind
o vento

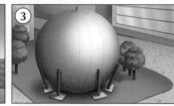

3. natural gas
o gás natural

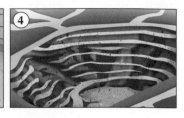

4. coal
o carvão

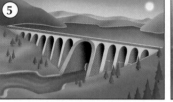

5. hydroelectric power
a energia hidroelétrica

6. oil / petroleum
o petróleo

7. geothermal energy
a energia geotérmica

8. nuclear energy
a energia nuclear

Pollution   Poluição

9. hazardous waste
os resíduos perigosos

10. air pollution / smog
a poluição do ar /
a névoa com poluição

11. acid rain
a chuva ácida

12. water pollution
a poluição da água

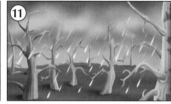

13. radiation
a radiação

14. pesticide poisoning
o envenenamento por agrotóxicos

15. oil spill
o derramamento de óleo

Conservation   Preservação

A. recycle
reciclar

B. save water / **conserve** water
economizar água

C. save energy / **conserve** energy
economizar energia

Share your answers.

1. How do you heat your home?
2. Do you have a gas stove or an electric stove?
3. What are some ways you can save energy when it's cold?
4. Do you recycle? What products do you recycle?
5. Does your market have recycling bins?

The Solar System

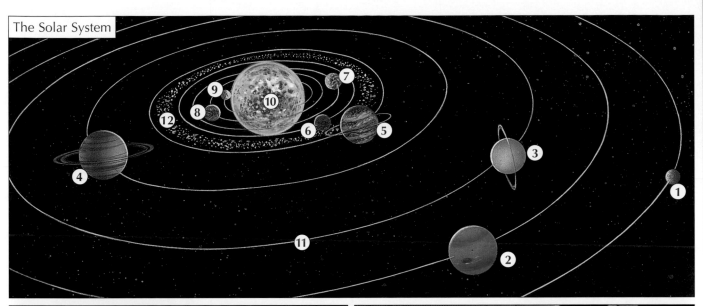

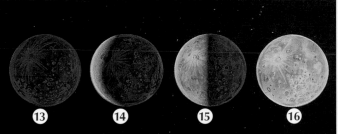

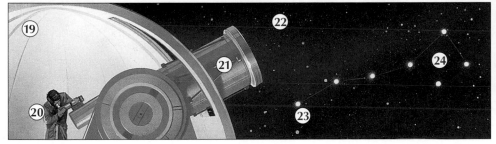

The planets
Os planetas

1. Pluto
   Plutão

2. Neptune
   Netuno

3. Uranus
   Urano

4. Saturn
   Saturno

5. Jupiter
   Júpiter

6. Mars
   Marte

7. Earth
   Terra

8. Venus
   Vênus

9. Mercury
   Mercúrio

10. sun
    o sol

11. orbit
    a órbita

12. asteroid belt
    o cinturão de asteróides

13. new moon
    a lua nova

14. crescent moon
    a lua crescente /
    o quarto crescente

15. quarter moon
    a lua minguante /
    o quarto minguante

16. full moon
    a lua cheia

17. astronaut
    o astronauta

18. space station
    a estação espacial

19. observatory
    o observatório

20. astronomer
    o astrônomo

21. telescope
    o telescópio

22. space
    o espaço

23. star
    a estrela

24. constellation
    a constelação

25. comet
    o cometa

26. galaxy
    a galáxia

More vocabulary

lunar eclipse: when the earth is between the sun and the moon

solar eclipse: when the moon is between the earth and the sun

Share your answers.

1. Do you know the names of any constellations?

2. How do you feel when you look up at the night sky?

3. Is the night sky in the U.S. the same as in your country?

Parts of a tree Partes de uma árvore

1. twig
o ramo (fino)

2. branch
o galho

3. limb
o limbo

4. trunk
o tronco

5. root
a raiz

6. leaf
a folha

7. redwood
(um tipo de) sequóia

8. birch
a bétula

9. magnolia
a magnólia

10. pine
o pinheiro

11. pinecone
a pinha

12. needle
a folha do pinheiro

13. maple
o ácer

14. willow
o salgueiro

15. palm
a palmeira

16. dogwood
o corniso

17. elm
o olmo

18. oak
o carvalho

Plants Plantas

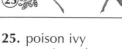

19. holly
o azevinho

20. berries
as frutas silvestres
(tipo amora)

21. cactus
o cacto

22. vine
a trepadeira

23. poison oak
o carvalho venenoso

24. poison sumac
o sumagre venenoso

25. poison ivy
o toxicoendro

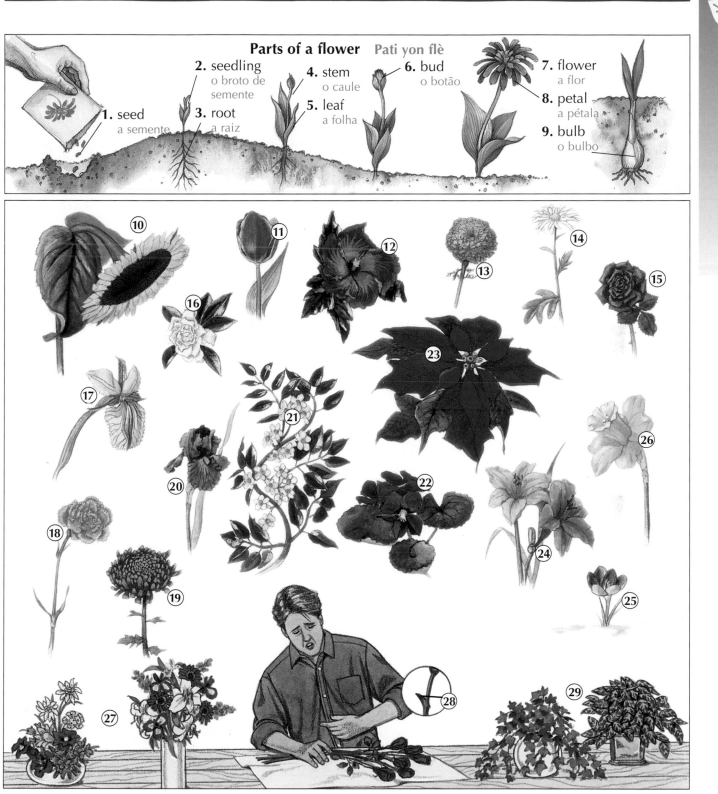

Parts of a flower Pati yon flè

1. seed
a semente

2. seedling
o broto de semente

3. root
a raiz

4. stem
o caule

5. leaf
a folha

6. bud
o botão

7. flower
a flor

8. petal
a pétala

9. bulb
o bulbo

10. sunflower
o girassol

11. tulip
a tulipa

12. hibiscus
o hibisco

13. marigold
o cravo-de-defunto

14. daisy
a margarida

15. rose
a rosa

16. gardenia
a gardênia

17. orchid
a orquídea

18. carnation
o cravo

19. chrysanthemum
o crisântemo

20. iris
a íris

21. jasmine
o jasmim

22. violet
a violeta

23. poinsettia
a flor-de-papagaio / a poinsétia

24. lily
o lírio

25. crocus
o açaflor (a flor do açafrão)

26. daffodil
o narciso

27. bouquet
o ramalhete

28. thorn
o espinho

29. houseplant
a planta de interiores

Parts of a fish Partes de um peixe

Sea animals Fauna marinha

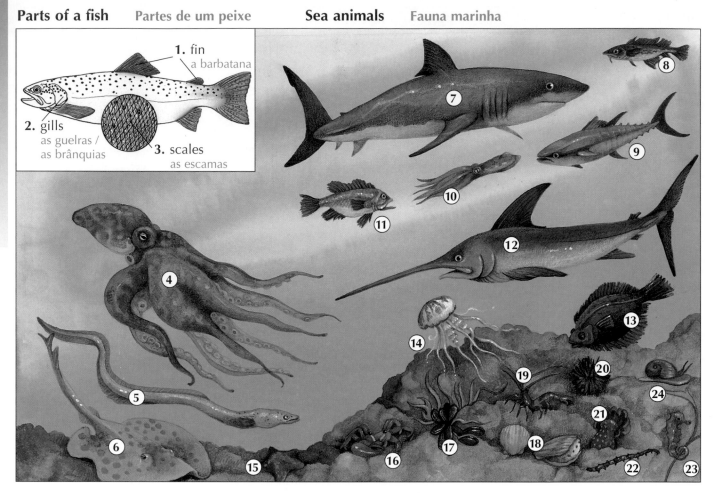

1. fin
   a barbatana
2. gills
   as guelras /
   as brânquias
3. scales
   as escamas

4. octopus
   o polvo
5. eel
   a enguia
6. ray
   a raia
7. shark
   o tubarão
8. cod
   o bacalhau
9. tuna
   o atum
10. squid
    a lula

11. bass
    a perca
12. swordfish
    o peixe-espada
13. flounder
    o linguado
14. jellyfish
    a água-viva
15. starfish
    a estrela-do-mar
16. crab
    o caranguejo
17. mussel
    o mexilhão

18. scallop
    a vieira
19. shrimp
    o camarão
20. sea urchin
    o ouriço-do-mar
21. sea anemone
    a anêmona-do-mar
22. worm
    a minhoca
23. sea horse
    o cavalo-marinho
24. snail
    o caramujo

Amphibians Anfíbios

25. frog
    a rã
26. newt
    a salamandra aquática
27. salamander
    a salamandra
28. toad
    o sapo

Sea mammals   Mamíferos marinhos

29. whale
a baleia

30. dolphin
o golfinho

31. porpoise
o boto

32. walrus
a morsa

33. seal
a foca

34. sea lion
o leão-marinho

35. otter
a lontra

Reptiles   Répteis

36. alligator
o jacaré

37. crocodile
o crocodilo

38. rattlesnake
a cascavel

39. garter snake
uma pequena cobra
não-venenosa

40. cobra
a naja

41. lizard
o lagarto

42. turtle
a tartaruga

Birds, Insects, and Arachnids   Pássaros, insetos e aracnídeos

Parts of a bird   Partes de um pássaro

1. beak / bill
   o bico
2. wing
   a asa
3. nest
   o ninho
4. claw
   a garra/a presa
5. feather
   a pena

6. owl a coruja	**9. woodpecker** o pica-pau	**12. penguin** o pingüim	**15. peacock** o pavão
7. blue jay o gaio	**10. eagle** a águia	**13. duck** o pato	**16. pigeon** a pomba
8. sparrow o pardal	**11. hummingbird** o beija-flor/o colibri	**14. goose** o ganso	**17. robin** o pintarroxo

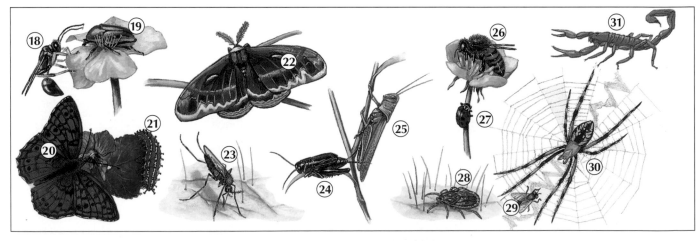

18. wasp a vespa	**22. moth** a mariposa	**25. grasshopper** o gafanhoto	**28. tick** o carrapato
19. beetle o besouro	**23. mosquito** o mosquito / o pernilongo	**26. honeybee** a abelha	**29. fly** a mosca
20. butterfly a borboleta	**24. cricket** o grilo	**27. ladybug** a joaninha	**30. spider** a aranha
21. caterpillar a lagarta			**31. scorpion** o escorpião

Farm animals   Animais de fazenda

1. goat
a cabra

2. donkey
o burro

3. cow
a vaca

4. horse
o cavalo

5. hen
a galinha

6. rooster
o galo

7. sheep
a ovelha

8. pig
o porco

Pets   Animais de estimação

9. cat
o gato

10. kitten
o filhote de gato

11. dog
o cachorro

12. puppy
o filhote de cachorro

13. rabbit
o coelho

14. guinea pig
o porquinho-da-índia

15. parakeet
o periquito

16. goldfish
o peixinho dourado

Rodents   Roedores

17. mouse
o camundongo

18. rat
o rato

19. gopher
o geômio

20. chipmunk
a tâmia (esquilo com dorso listado)

21. squirrel
o esquilo

22. prairie dog
a marmota

More vocabulary

Wild animals live, eat, and raise their young away from people, in the forests, mountains, plains, etc.

Domesticated animals work for people or live with them.

Share your answers.

1. Do you have any pets? any farm animals?

2. Which of these animals are in your neighborhood? Which are not?

1. moose
   o alce

2. mountain lion
   o puma

3. coyote
   o coiote

4. opossum
   o gambá norte-americano

5. wolf
   o lobo

6. buffalo / bison
   o búfalo / o bisão

7. bat
   o morcego

8. armadillo
   o tatu

9. beaver
   o castor

10. porcupine
    o porco-espinho

11. bear
    o urso

12. skunk
    o gambá

13. raccoon
    o guaxinim /
    o mão-pelada

14. deer
    o veado

15. fox
    a raposa

16. antler
    a galhada

17. hoof
    o casco

18. whiskers
    o bigode

19. coat / fur
    o pêlo / a pele

20. paw
    a pata

21. horn
    o chifre

22. tail
    o rabo / a cauda

23. quill
    o espinho

24. anteater
o tamanduá

25. leopard
o leopardo

26. llama
a lhama

27. monkey
o macaco

28. chimpanzee
o chimpanzé

29. rhinoceros
o rinoceronte

30. gorilla
o gorila

31. hyena
a hiena

32. baboon
o babuíno

33. giraffe
a girafa

34. zebra
a zebra

35. antelope
o antílope

36. lion
o leão

37. tiger
o tigre

38. camel
o camelo

39. panther
a pantera

40. orangutan
o orangotango

41. panda
o panda

42. elephant
o elefante

43. hippopotamus
o hipopótamo

44. kangaroo
o canguru

45. koala
o coala

46. platypus
o ornitorrinco

47. trunk
a tromba

48. tusk
a presa

49. mane
a juba

50. pouch
a bolsa

51. hump
a corcova

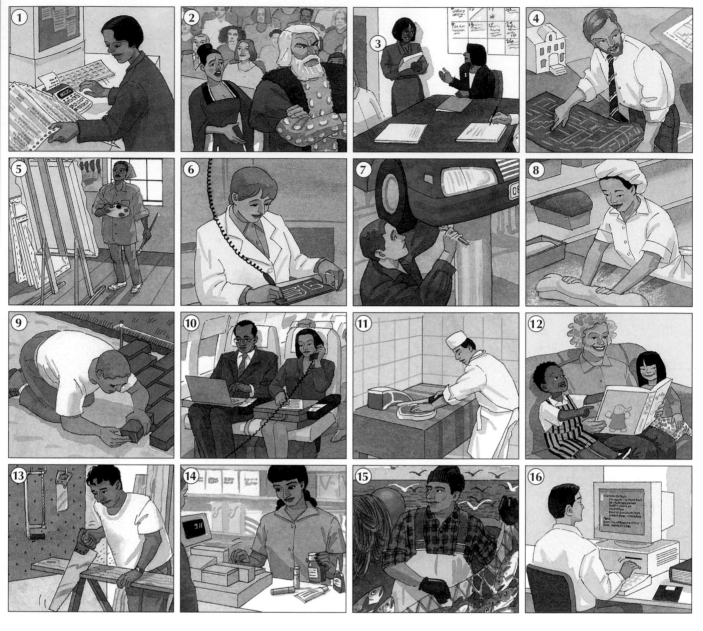

1. accountant
   a contadora

2. actor
   o ator / a atriz

3. administrative assistant
   a assistente administrativa

4. architect
   o arquiteto

5. artist
   o artista

6. assembler
   a montadora

7. auto mechanic
   o mecânico de automóveis

8. baker
   a padeira

9. bricklayer
   o pedreiro

10. businessman/businesswoman
    o homem / a mulher de negócios

11. butcher
    o açougueiro

12. caregiver/baby-sitter
    a babá

13. carpenter
    o carpinteiro

14. cashier
    a caixa

15. commercial fisher
    o pescador profissional

16. computer programmer
    o programador de computador

Use the new language.

1. Who works outside?

2. Who works inside?

3. Who makes things?

4. Who uses a computer?

5. Who wears a uniform?

6. Who sells things?

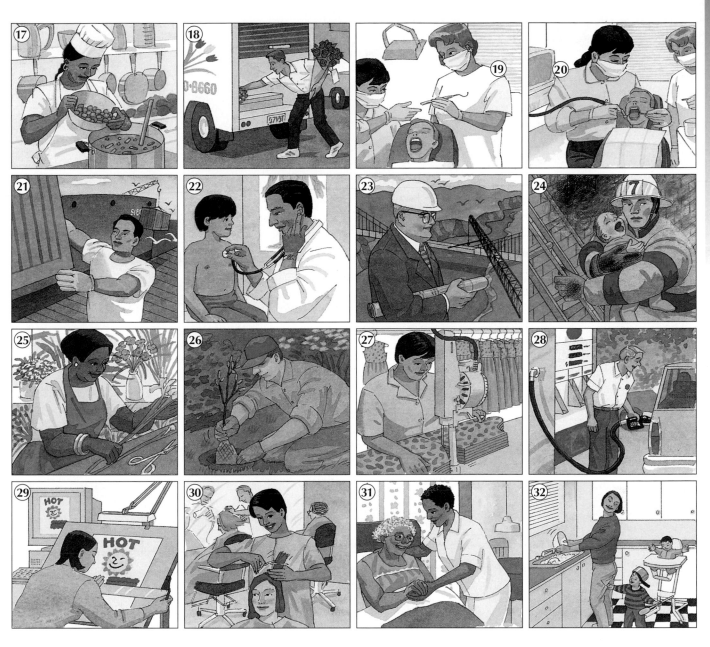

17. cook
    a cozinheira

18. delivery person
    o entregador

19. dental assistant
    a assistente de dentista

20. dentist
    a dentista

21. dockworker
    o estivador

22. doctor
    o médico

23. engineer
    o engenheiro

24. firefighter
    o bombeiro

25. florist
    a florista

26. gardener
    o jardineiro

27. garment worker
    a funcionária de confecção

28. gas station attendant
    o frentista

29. graphic artist
    a desenhista gráfica

30. hairdresser
    a cabeleireira

31. home attendant
    a enfermeira particular

32. homemaker
    a dona de casa

Share your answers.

1. Do you know people who have some of these jobs? What do they say about their work?

2. Which of these jobs are available in your city?

3. For which of these jobs do you need special training?

33. **housekeeper**
   a empregada doméstica

34. **interpreter/translator**
   o intérprete / o tradutor

35. **janitor/custodian**
   o zelador

36. **lawyer**
   o advogado

37. **machine operator**
   a operadora de máquina

38. **messenger/courier**
   o mensageiro

39. **model**
   a modelo

40. **mover**
   o carregador de mudança

41. **musician**
   o músico

42. **nurse**
   a enfermeira

43. **painter**
   o pintor

44. **police officer**
   a policial

45. **postal worker**
   a funcionária do correio

46. **printer**
   o tipógrafo / o impressor

47. **receptionist**
   a recepcionista

48. **repair person**
   o técnico

Talk about each of the jobs or occupations.

She's _a housekeeper_. She works in _a hotel_.

He's _an interpreter_. He works for _the government_.

She's _a nurse_. She works with _patients_.

49. reporter
    o repórter

50. salesclerk / salesperson
    o balconista / o vendedor

51. sanitation worker
    o lixeiro

52. secretary
    a secretária

53. server
    a garçonete

54. serviceman / servicewoman
    o / a recruta

55. stock clerk
    o almoxarife

56. store owner
    a comerciante

57. student
    a estudante

58. teacher / instructor
    a professora / a instrutora

59. telemarketer
    o operador de telemarketing

60. travel agent
    o agente de viagem

61. truck driver
    o caminhoneiro

62. veterinarian
    a médica veterinária

63. welder
    o soldador

64. writer / author
    o escritor / o autor

Talk about your job or the job you want.

What do you do?

  I'm a salesclerk. I work in a store.

What do you want to do?

  I want to be a veterinarian. I want to work with animals.

A. **assemble** components
montar componentes

B. **assist** medical patients
auxiliar pacientes

C. **cook**
cozinhar

D. **do** manual labor
fazer trabalho braçal

E. **drive** a truck
dirigir um caminhão

F. **operate** heavy machinery
operar máquinas pesadas

G. **repair** appliances
consertar eletrodomésticos

H. **sell** cars
vender carros

I. **sew** clothes
costurar roupas

J. **speak** another language
falar outro idioma

K. **supervise** people
supervisionar outras pessoas

L. **take care** of children
cuidar de crianças

M. **type**
datilografar / digitar

N. **use** a cash register
operar uma caixa registradora

O. **wait on** customers
atender os clientes

P. **work** on a computer
trabalhar com computador

More vocabulary

act: to perform in a play, movie, or TV show

fly: to pilot an airplane

teach: to instruct, to show how to do something

Share your answers.

1. What job skills do you have? Where did you learn them?

2. What job skills do you want to learn?

A. talk to friends
conversar com amigos

B. look at a job board
olhar no mural de empregos

C. look for a help wanted sign
procurar placas de "Precisa-se"

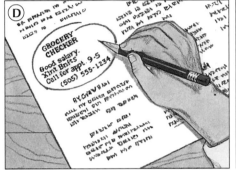

D. look in the classifieds
procurar nos classificados

E. call for information
ligar para obter informações

F. ask about the hours
perguntar sobre o horário

G. fill out an application
preencher uma ficha de emprego

H. go on an interview
ir a uma entrevista

I. talk about your experience
falar sobre a sua experiência

J. ask about benefits
perguntar sobre os benefícios

K. inquire about the salary
perguntar sobre o salário

L. get hired
ser admitido

141

An Office   Um escritório

1. **desk**
   a escrivaninha

2. **typewriter**
   a máquina de escrever

3. **secretary**
   a secretária

4. **microcassette transcriber**
   um microgravador para transcrição

5. **stacking tray**
   as bandejas de entrada e saída

6. **desk calendar**
   o calendário de mesa

7. **desk pad**
   o risque e rabisque

8. **calculator**
   a calculadora

9. **electric pencil sharpener**
   o apontador elétrico de lápis

10. **file cabinet**
    o arquivo

11. **file folder**
    a pasta de arquivo

12. **file clerk**
    o arquivista

13. **supply cabinet**
    o armário para materiais de escritório

14. **photocopier**
    a máquina fotocopiadora

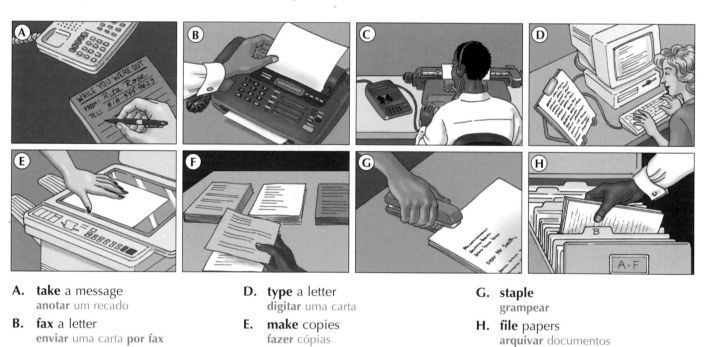

A. **take** a message
   anotar um recado

B. **fax** a letter
   enviar uma carta **por fax**

C. **transcribe** notes
   transcrever anotações

D. **type** a letter
   digitar uma carta

E. **make** copies
   fazer cópias

F. **collate** papers
   organizar os documentos

G. **staple**
   grampear

H. **file** papers
   arquivar documentos

Practice taking messages.

Hello. My name is <u>Sara Scott</u>. Is <u>Mr. Lee</u> in?

   Not yet. Would you like to leave a message?

Yes. Please ask <u>him</u> to call me at <u>555-4859</u>.

Share your answers.

1. Which office equipment do you know how to use?
2. Which jobs does a file clerk do?
3. Which jobs does a secretary do?

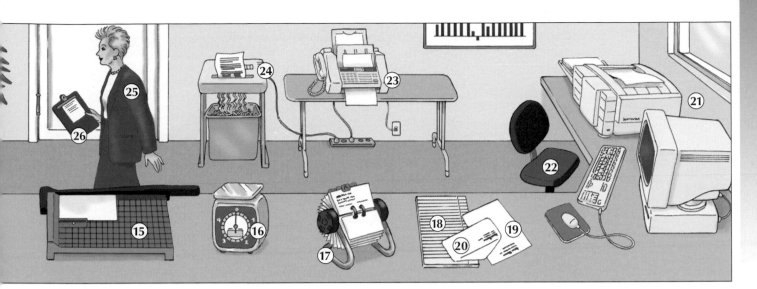

15. paper cutter
a guilhotina

16. postal scale
a balança postal

17. rotary card file
o rolodex

18. legal pad
o bloco tamanho ofício

19. letterhead paper
o papel timbrado

20. envelope
o envelope

21. computer workstation
a estação de trabalho de computador

22. swivel chair
a cadeira giratória

23. fax machine
o aparelho de fax

24. paper shredder
o triturador de papéis

25. office manager
a chefe de escritório

26. clipboard
a prancheta

27. appointment book
a agenda

28. stapler
o grampeador

29. staple
o grampo

30. organizer
a agenda organizadora / geral

31. typewriter cartridge
o cartucho de fita para máquina de escrever

32. mailer
o "petit-paquet"

33. correction fluid
o líquido corretivo / o corretor líquido

34. Post-it notes
o post-it / o papel-lembrete adesivo

35. label
a etiqueta

36. notepad
o bloco de anotações

37. glue
a cola

38. rubber cement
a goma arábica

39. clear tape
a fita adesiva transparente

40. rubber stamp
o carimbo de borracha

41. ink pad
a almofada para carimbo

42. packing tape
a fita adesiva de PVC (para empacotar)

43. pushpin
o percevejo / a tacha

44. paper clip
o clipe

45. rubber band
o elástico

Use the new language.

1. Which items keep things together?

2. Which items are used to mail packages?

3. Which items are made of paper?

Share your answers.

1. Which office supplies do students use?

2. Where can you buy them?

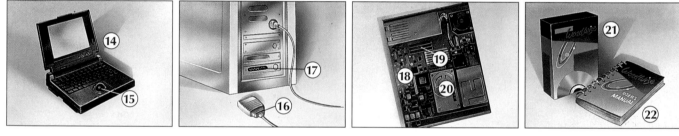

Hardware
Hardware / Equipamentos e periféricos

1. **CPU** (central processing unit)
   a CPU (unidade central de processamento)

2. **CD-ROM** disc
   o CD-ROM

3. **disk drive**
   a unidade de disco

4. **power switch**
   o comutador liga / desliga

5. **disk / floppy**
   o disquete / o disco flexível

6. **monitor / screen**
   o monitor / a tela

7. **keyboard**
   o teclado

8. **mouse**
   o mouse

9. **joystick**
   o joystick

10. **surge protector**
    o filtro de linha

11. **modem**
    o modem

12. **printer**
    a impressora

13. **scanner**
    o scanner

14. **laptop**
    o computador portátil (notebook)

15. **trackball**
    o trackball

16. **cable**
    o cabo

17. **port**
    a porta

18. **motherboard**
    a placa-mãe

19. **slot**
    o slot / a abertura

20. **hard disk drive**
    a unidade de disco rígido

Software
Software/Programas

21. **program / application**
    o programa / o aplicativo

22. **user's manual**
    o manual do usuário

More vocabulary

data: information that a computer can read

memory: how much data a computer can hold

speed: how fast a computer can work with data

Share your answers.

1. Can you use a computer?

2. How did you learn? in school? from a book? by yourself?

1. valet parking
   o serviço de manobrista

2. doorman
   o porteiro

3. lobby
   o saguão

4. bell captain
   o chefe dos carregadores

5. bellhop
   o carregador de bagagem

6. luggage cart
   o carrinho de bagagem

7. gift shop
   a loja de presentes

8. front desk
   a recepção

9. desk clerk
   o recepcionista

10. guest room
    o quarto de hóspedes

11. guest
    o hóspede

12. room service
    o serviço de quarto

13. hall
    o corredor

14. housekeeping cart
    o carrinho de limpeza

15. housekeeper
    a camareira

16. pool
    a piscina

17. pool service
    o serviço de limpeza de piscina

18. ice machine
    a máquina de gelo

19. meeting room
    a sala de conferência

20. ballroom
    o salão de festas

More vocabulary

concierge: the hotel worker who helps guests find restaurants and interesting places to go

service elevator: an elevator for hotel workers

Share your answers.

1. Does this look like a hotel in your city? Which one?

2. Which hotel job is the most difficult?

3. How much does it cost to stay in a hotel in your city?

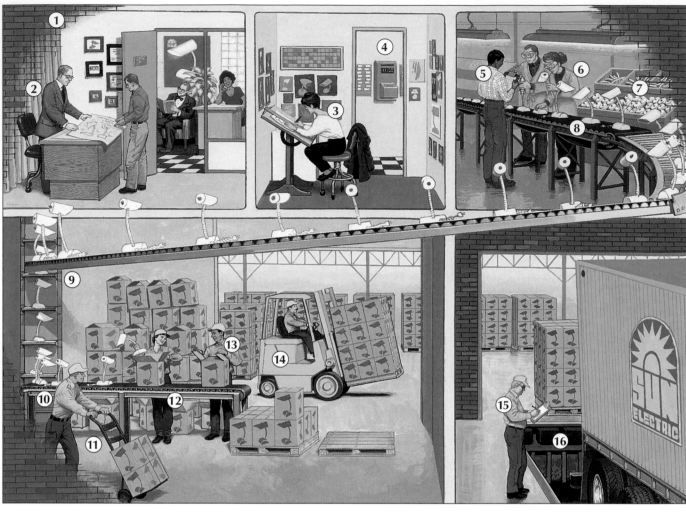

1. **front office**
   o escritório principal /
   a administração

2. **factory owner**
   o dono da fábrica

3. **designer**
   a projetista

4. **time clock**
   o relógio de ponto

5. **line supervisor**
   o supervisor de linha de montagem

6. **factory worker**
   o(a) operário(a)

7. **parts**
   as peças

8. **assembly line**
   a linha de montagem

9. **warehouse**
   o depósito

10. **order puller**
    o encarregado de pedidos

11. **hand truck**
    o carrinho de mão

12. **conveyor belt**
    a esteira transportadora

13. **packer**
    o(a) empacotador(a)

14. **forklift**
    a empilhadeira

15. **shipping clerk**
    o encarregado da expedição

16. **loading dock**
    a plataforma de carga

A. **design**
   projetar

B. **manufacture**
   fabricar

C. **ship**
   despachar

146

1. electrical hazard
   perigo: eletricidade
2. flammable
   inflamável
3. poison
   veneno
4. corrosive
   corrosivo
5. biohazard
   perigo devido a substâncias
   biológicas
6. radioactive
   radioativo
7. hazardous materials
   materiais perigosos
8. dangerous situation
   condições perigosas

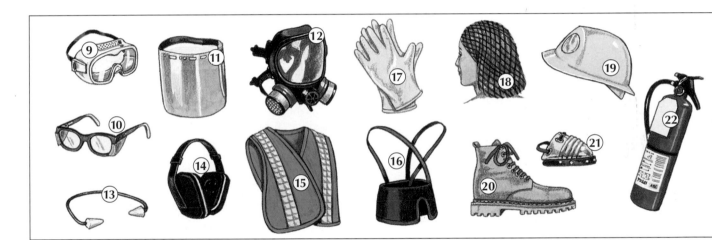

9. safety goggles
   a máscara de proteção
10. safety glasses
    os óculos de proteção
11. safety visor
    a máscara de soldador
12. respirator
    o respirador / a máscara antigás
13. earplugs
    o protetor / o plugue de ouvido
14. safety earmuffs
    o protetor de orelha
15. safety vest
    o colete de proteção
16. back support
    o suporte para costas
17. latex gloves
    as luvas de borracha
18. hair net
    a rede para cabelo
19. hard hat
    o capacete de proteção
20. safety boot
    a bota de proteção
21. toe guard
    a proteção para os dedos dos pés
22. fire extinguisher
    o extintor de incêndio

23. careless
    descuidado
24. careful
    cuidadoso

Crops   Plantações

1. **rice**
   o arroz

2. **wheat**
   o trigo

3. **soybeans**
   a soja

4. **corn**
   o milho

5. **alfalfa**
   a alfafa

6. **cotton**
   o algodão

7. **field**
   o campo

8. **farmworker**
   o trabalhador agrícola

9. **tractor**
   o trator

10. **farm equipment**
    o equipamento agrícola

11. **barn**
    o celeiro

12. **vegetable garden**
    a horta

13. **livestock**
    o gado

14. **vineyard**
    o vinhedo / a vinha

15. **farmer / grower**
    o fazendeiro / o agricultor

16. **orchard**
    o pomar

17. **corral**
    o curral

18. **hay**
    o feno

19. **fence**
    a cerca

20. **hired hand**
    o bóia-fria

21. **steers / cattle**
    os novilhos / o gado

22. **rancher**
    o boiadeiro

A. **plant**
   plantar

B. **harvest**
   colher

C. **milk**
   ordenhar

D. **feed**
   alimentar

1. **construction worker**
   o trabalhador de construção

2. **ladder**
   a escada de pedreiro

3. **I beam / girder**
   a viga(-mestra)

4. **scaffolding**
   o andaime

5. **cherry picker**
   o guindaste de cesta

6. **bulldozer**
   o trator de terraplanagem

7. **crane**
   o guindaste

8. **backhoe**
   a retroescavadeira

9. **jackhammer / pneumatic drill**
   a broca pneumática / a britadeira

10. **concrete**
    o concreto

11. **bricks**
    os tijolos

12. **trowel**
    a colher de pedreiro

13. **insulation**
    a manta isolante / o material isolante

14. **stucco**
    o estuque

15. **window pane**
    o vidro / a vidraça

16. **plywood**
    a madeira compensada

17. **wood / lumber**
    a madeira / a madeira de construção

18. **drywall**
    a parede construída sem argamassa

19. **shingles**
    as telhas de madeira

20. **pickax**
    a picareta

21. **shovel**
    a pá

22. **sledgehammer**
    a marreta

A. **paint**
   pintar

B. **lay** bricks
   assentar tijolos

C. **measure**
   medir

D. **hammer**
   martelar / pregar

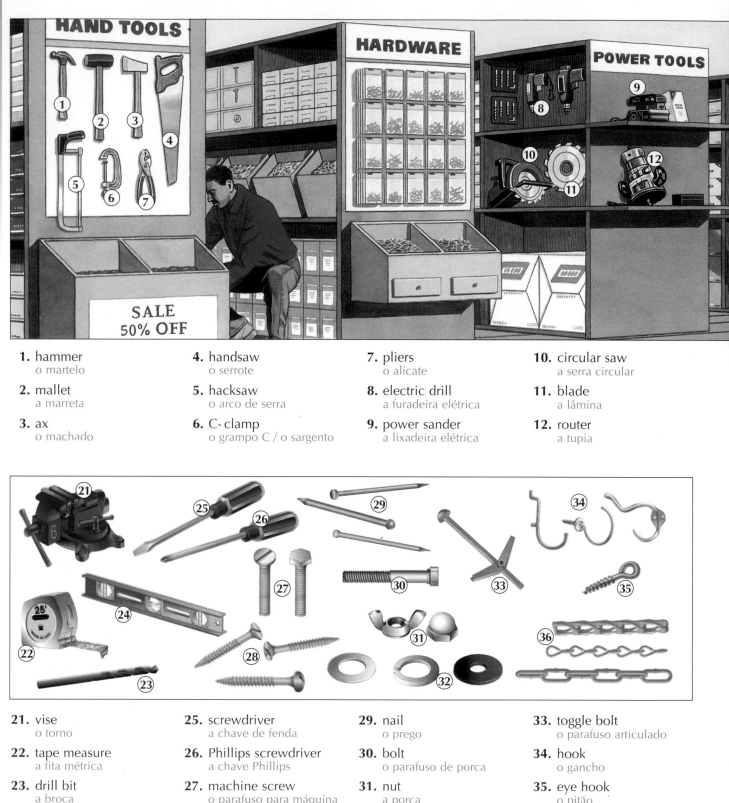

1. hammer
o martelo

2. mallet
a marreta

3. ax
o machado

4. handsaw
o serrote

5. hacksaw
o arco de serra

6. C-clamp
o grampo C / o sargento

7. pliers
o alicate

8. electric drill
a furadeira elétrica

9. power sander
a lixadeira elétrica

10. circular saw
a serra circular

11. blade
a lâmina

12. router
a tupia

21. vise
o torno

22. tape measure
a fita métrica

23. drill bit
a broca

24. level
o nível

25. screwdriver
a chave de fenda

26. Phillips screwdriver
a chave Phillips

27. machine screw
o parafuso para máquina

28. wood screw
o parafuso para madeira

29. nail
o prego

30. bolt
o parafuso de porca

31. nut
a porca

32. washer
a arruela

33. toggle bolt
o parafuso articulado

34. hook
o gancho

35. eye hook
o pitão

36. chain
a corrente

Use the new language.

1. Which tools are used for plumbing?

2. Which tools are used for painting?

3. Which tools are used for electrical work?

4. Which tools are used for working with wood?

13. wire
o fio

14. extension cord
a extensão

15. yardstick
a régua de uma jarda

16. pipe
o tubo / o cano

17. fittings
as conexões

18. wood
a madeira

19. spray gun
a pistola de pintura

20. paint
a tinta

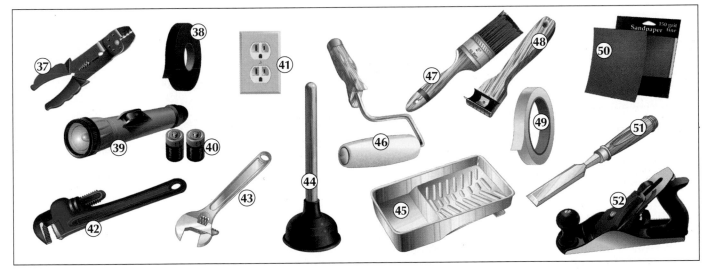

37. wire stripper
os alicates para
descascar fios

38. electrical tape
a fita isolante

39. flashlight
a lanterna

40. battery
a bateria

41. outlet
a tomada

42. pipe wrench
a chave de grifo

43. wrench
a chave inglesa

44. plunger
o desentupidor

45. paint pan
a bandeja de pintura

46. paint roller
o rolo de pintar

47. paintbrush
o pincel

48. scraper
o raspador

49. masking tape
a fita de arremate

50. sandpaper
a lixa

51. chisel
o formão

52. plane
a plaina

Use the new language.

Look at **Household Problems and Repairs,**
pages **48–49.**

Name the tools you use to fix the problems you see.

Share your answers.

1. Which tools do you have in your home?

2. Which tools can be dangerous to use?

Places to Go   Lugares para passear

1. **zoo**
   o jardim zoológico

2. **animals**
   os animais

3. **zookeeper**
   o funcionário do zoológico

4. **botanical gardens**
   o jardim botânico

5. **greenhouse**
   a estufa

6. **gardener**
   o jardineiro

7. **art museum**
   o museu de arte

8. **painting**
   a pintura

9. **sculpture**
   a escultura

10. **the movies**
    o cinema

11. **seat**
    a poltrona

12. **screen**
    a tela

13. **amusement park**
    o parque de diversões

14. **puppet show**
    o teatro de marionetes

15. **roller coaster**
    a montanha russa

16. **carnival**
    o parque de diversões (itinerante)

17. **rides**
    as atrações

18. **game**
    o jogo

19. **county fair**
    a feira / a exposição de cidade de interior

20. **first place/first prize**
    o primeiro lugar / o primeiro prêmio

21. **exhibition**
    a exposição

22. **swap meet/flea market**
    o bazar / o mercado das pulgas

23. **booth**
    a barraca de feira

24. **merchandise**
    a mercadoria

25. **baseball game**
    o jogo de beisebol

26. **stadium**
    o estádio

27. **announcer**
    o locutor

Talk about the places you like to go.

I like _animals_, so I go to _the zoo_.
I like _rides_, so I go to _carnivals_.

Share your answers.

1. Which of these places is interesting to you?
2. Which rides do you like at an amusement park?
3. What are some famous places to go to in your country?

152

1. **ball field**
   o campo (de jogar bola)

2. **bike path**
   a ciclovia

3. **cyclist**
   o ciclista

4. **bicycle/bike**
   a bicicleta

5. **jump rope**
   a corda de pular

6. **duck pond**
   o lago dos patos

7. **tennis court**
   a quadra de tênis

8. **picnic table**
   a mesa de piquenique

9. **tricycle**
   o triciclo / o velocípede

10. **bench**
    o banco (de jardim)

11. **water fountain**
    o bebedouro

12. **swings**
    os balanços

13. **slide**
    o escorregador

14. **climbing apparatus**
    o trepa-trepa

15. **sandbox**
    o tanque de areia

16. **seesaw**
    a gangorra

A. **pull** the wagon
   puxar o carrinho

B. **push** the swing
   empurrar o balanço

C. **climb** on the bars
   escalar as barras

D. **picnic/have** a picnic
   fazer um piquenique

Outdoor Recreation Recreação ao ar livre

1. **camping**
   o acampamento

2. **boating**
   o passeio de barco

3. **canoeing**
   o passeio de canoa/a canoagem

4. **rafting**
   o passeio de bote inflável

5. **fishing**
   a pescaria

6. **hiking**
   a caminhada

7. **backpacking**
   viajar de mochila

8. **mountain biking**
   o ciclismo de montanha /
   andar de mountain bike

9. **horseback riding**
   andar a cavalo / equitação

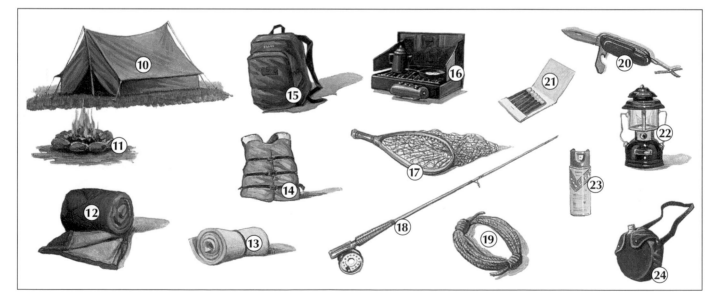

10. **tent**
    a barraca

11. **campfire**
    a fogueira

12. **sleeping bag**
    o saco de dormir

13. **foam pad**
    o colchonete

14. **life vest**
    o colete salva-vidas

15. **backpack**
    a mochila

16. **camping stove**
    o fogareiro

17. **fishing net**
    a rede de pesca / o puçá

18. **fishing pole**
    a vara de pescar

19. **rope**
    a corda

20. **multi-use knife**
    o canivete multiuso / suíço

21. **matches**
    os fósforos

22. **lantern**
    a lanterna

23. **insect repellent**
    o repelente de insetos

24. **canteen**
    o cantil

1. ocean / water o mar / a água	**9.** beach umbrella o guarda-sol	**17.** sunbather o(a) banhista
2. fins a nadadeira / o pé-de-pato	**10.** sand castle o castelo de areia	**18.** lifeguard o salva-vidas
3. diving mask a máscara de mergulho	**11.** cooler a caixa de isopor	**19.** lifesaving device o equipamento salva-vidas
4. sailboat o veleiro	**12.** shade a sombra	**20.** lifeguard station o posto salva-vidas
5. surfboard a prancha de surfe	**13.** sunscreen / sunblock o protetor solar / o bloqueador solar	**21.** seashell a concha
6. wave a onda	**14.** beach chair a cadeira de praia	**22.** pail / bucket o baldinho
7. wet suit a roupa de mergulho	**15.** beach towel a toalha de praia	**23.** sand a areia
8. scuba tank o tanque / o cilindro de oxigênio	**16.** pier o píer	**24.** rock a pedra

More vocabulary

seaweed: a plant that grows in the ocean

tide: the level of the ocean. The tide goes in and out every twelve hours.

Share your answers.

1. Are there any beaches near your home?

2. Do you prefer to spend more time on the sand or in the water?

3. Where are some of the world's best beaches?

155

Sports Verbs   Verbos utilizados em esportes

A. **walk**
andar

B. **jog**
fazer cooper

C. **run**
correr

D. **throw**
jogar

E. **catch**
pegar

F. **pitch**
lançar / atirar

G. **hit**
bater

H. **pass**
passar

I. **shoot**
arremessar

J. **jump**
pular

K. **dribble / bounce**
driblar / bater (bola)

L. **kick**
chutar

M. **tackle**
atacar / agarrar

Practice talking about what you can do.

I can swim, but I can't dive.

I can pass the ball well, but I can't shoot too well.

Use the new language.

Look at **Individual Sports,** page **159.**

Name the actions you see people doing.

The man in number 18 is riding a horse.

N. **serve**
sacar

O. **swing**
girar / brandir

P. **exercise / work out**
exercitar / malhar

Q. **stretch**
esticar / alongar

R. **bend**
flexionar / curvar

S. **dive**
mergulhar

T. **swim**
nadar

U. **ski**
esquiar

V. **skate**
patinar

W. **ride**
andar de bicicleta

X. **start**
começar / largar

Y. **race**
competir em
uma corrida

Z. **finish**
terminar / chegar

Share your answers.

1. What do you like to do?
2. What do you have difficulty doing?

3. How often do you exercise? Once a week? Two or three times a week? More? Never?
4. Which is more difficult, throwing a ball or catching it?

1. **score**
   o placar

2. **coach**
   o técnico / o treinador

3. **team**
   o time / a equipe

4. **fan**
   o torcedor

5. **player**
   o jogador

6. **official / referee**
   o juiz / o árbitro

7. **basketball court**
   a quadra de basquete

8. **basketball**
   o basquete

9. **baseball**
   o beisebol

10. **softball**
    o softball

11. **football**
    o futebol americano

12. **soccer**
    o futebol

13. **ice hockey**
    o hóquei sobre gelo

14. **volleyball**
    o voleibol

15. **water polo**
    o pólo aquático

More vocabulary

captain: the team leader

umpire: in baseball, the name for the referee

Little League: a baseball league for children

win: to have the best score

lose: the opposite of win

tie: to have the same score as the other team

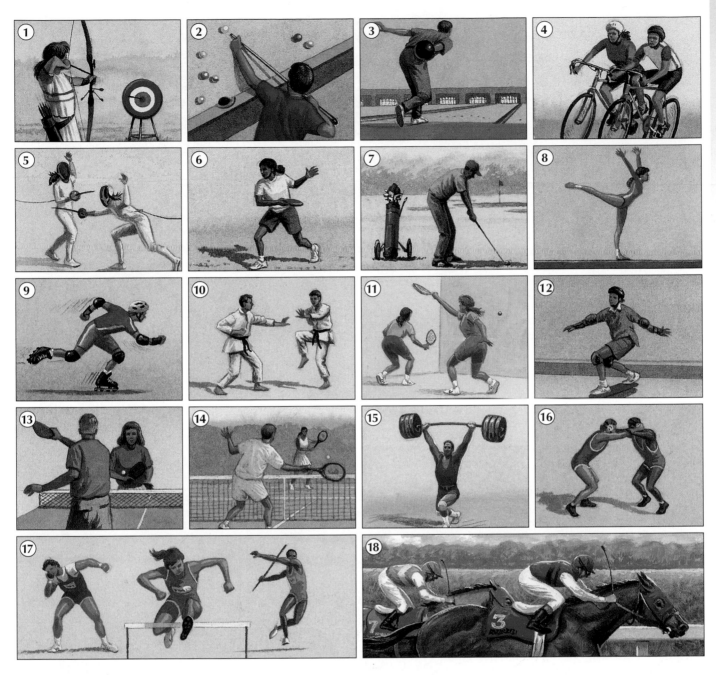

1. **archery**
   o arco e flecha

2. **billiards/pool**
   o bilhar / a sinuca

3. **bowling**
   o boliche

4. **cycling/biking**
   o ciclismo

5. **fencing**
   a esgrima

6. **flying disc***
   brincar de lançar disco

7. **golf**
   o golfe

8. **gymnastics**
   a ginástica olímpica

9. **inline skating**
   a patinação inline

10. **martial arts**
    as artes marciais

11. **racquetball**
    o racquetball

12. **skateboarding**
    o skate

13. **table tennis/
    Ping-Pong™**
    o tênis de mesa /
    o pingue-pongue

14. **tennis**
    o tênis

15. **weightlifting**
    o halterofilismo

16. **wrestling**
    a luta romana

17. **track and field**
    o atletismo

18. **horse racing**
    o hipismo / o turfe

***Note:** One brand is Frisbee®
(Mattel, Inc.)

Talk about sports.

Which sports do you like?

I like <u>tennis</u> but I don't like <u>golf</u>.

Share your answers.

1. Which sports are good for children to learn? Why?

2. Which sport is the most difficult to learn? Why?

3. Which sport is the most dangerous? Why?

1. downhill skiing
o esqui de descida / alpino

2. snowboarding
o snowboard / o skate na neve

3. cross-country skiing
o esqui de fundo / o esqui nórdico

4. ice skating
a patinação no gelo

5. figure skating
a patinação artística

6. sledding
o passeio de trenó

7. waterskiing
o esqui aquático

8. sailing
o iatismo

9. surfing
o surfe

10. sailboarding
o surfe a vela / o windsurf

11. snorkeling
o mergulho com snorkel

12. scuba diving
o mergulho scuba / com tanque
de oxigênio

Use the new language.
Look at **The Beach,** page 155.
Name the sports you see.

Share your answers.
1. Which sports are in the Winter Olympics?
2. Which sports do you think are the most exciting
   to watch?

1. golf club
   o taco de golfe

2. tennis racket
   a raquete de tênis

3. volleyball
   a bola de vôlei

4. basketball
   a bola de basquete

5. bowling ball
   a bola de boliche

6. bow
   o arco

7. arrow
   a flecha

8. target
   o alvo

9. ice skates
   os patins para gelo

10. inline skates
    os patins inline

11. hockey stick
    o bastão de hóquei

12. soccer ball
    a bola de futebol

13. shin guards
    a caneleira

14. baseball bat
    o taco de beisebol

15. catcher's mask
    a máscara do apanhador

16. uniform
    o uniforme

17. glove
    a luva

18. baseball
    a bola de beisebol

19. weights
    os pesos

20. football helmet
    o capacete de
    futebol americano

21. shoulder pads
    as ombreiras

22. football
    a bola de
    futebol americano

23. snowboard
    o snowboard /
    a prancha de neve

24. skis
    os esquis

25. ski poles
    os bastões de esqui

26. ski boots
    as botas de esqui

27. flying disc*
    o disco (tipo Frisbee®)

*Note: One brand is Frisbee®
(Mattel, Inc.)

Share your answers.

1. Which sports equipment is used for safety reasons?

2. Which sports equipment is heavy?

3. What sports equipment do you have at home?

Use the new language.

Look at **Individual Sports,** page **159.**

Name the sports equipment you see.

A. **collect** things
colecionar objetos

B. **play** games
participar de jogos /
jogar

C. **build** models
construir modelos

D. **do** crafts
fazer artesanato

1. video game system
o jogo de videogame

2. cartridge
o cartucho

3. board game
o jogo de tabuleiro

4. dice
os dados

5. checkers
o jogo de damas

6. chess
o jogo de xadrez

7. model kit
o kit de aeromodelismo

8. glue
a cola

9. acrylic paint
a tinta acrílica

10. figurine
a miniatura (de pessoa)

11. baseball card
os cartões / as figurinhas
de beisebol

12. stamp collection
a coleção de selos

13. coin collection
a coleção de moedas

14. clay
a massa de modelar

15. doll making kit
o kit para fazer bonecas

16. woodworking kit
o kit para artesanato
de madeira / para
marcenaria

Talk about how much time you spend on your hobbies.

I *do crafts* all the time.

I *play chess* sometimes.

I never *build models*.

Share your answers.

1. How often do you play video games? Often?
Sometimes? Never?

2. What board games do you know?

3. Do you collect anything? What?

E. paint
pintar

F. knit
tricotar

G. pretend
fazer de conta

H. play cards
jogar baralho

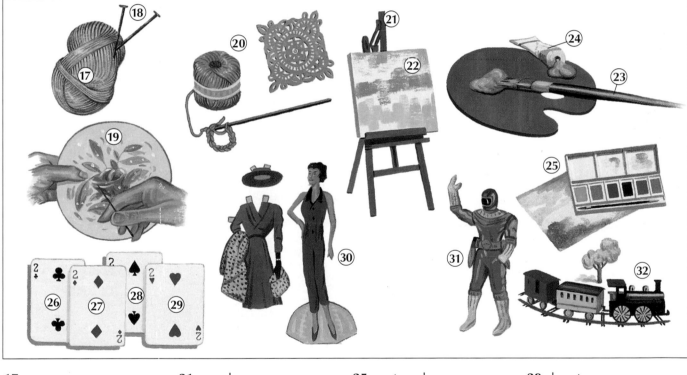

17. yarn
a novelo (de lã)

18. knitting needles
as agulhas de tricô

19. embroidery
o bordado

20. crochet
o crochê

21. easel
o cavalete

22. canvas
a tela

23. paintbrush
o pincel

24. oil paint
a tinta a óleo

25. watercolor
a aquarela

26. clubs
paus

27. diamonds
ouros

28. spades
espadas

29. hearts
copas

30. paper doll
a boneca de papel

31. action figure
o herói de aventura

32. model trains
o trenzinho

Share your answers.

1. Do you like to play cards? Which games?

2. Did you pretend a lot when you were a child? What did you pretend to be?

3. Is it important to have hobbies? Why or why not?

4. What's your favorite game?

5. What's your hobby?

1. **clock radio**
   o rádio-relógio

2. **portable radio-cassette player**
   o rádio-gravador portátil

3. **cassette recorder**
   o gravador

4. **microphone**
   o microfone

5. **shortwave radio**
   o rádio de ondas curtas

6. **TV (television)**
   a TV (o televisor)

7. **portable TV**
   o televisor portátil

8. **VCR (videocassette recorder)**
   o videocassete

9. **remote control**
   o controle remoto

10. **videocassette**
    a fita de vídeo

11. **speakers**
    a caixa acústica

12. **turntable**
    o toca-disco

13. **tuner**
    o sintonizador

14. **CD player**
    o CD player

15. **personal radio-cassette player**
    o walkman

16. **headphones**
    os fones de ouvido

17. **adapter**
    o plugue

18. **plug**
    o adaptador

19. video camera
a câmera de vídeo

20. tripod
o tripé

21. camcorder
a câmera camcorder

22. battery pack
a bateria

23. battery charger
o carregador de bateria

24. 35 mm camera
a câmera de 35 mm

25. zoom lens
a lente de zoom / a teleobjetiva

26. film
o filme

27. camera case
a maleta / a bolsa térmica

28. screen
a tela

29. carousel slide projector
o projetor de slide

30. slide tray
o carrossel para slides

31. slides
os slides

32. photo album
o álbum de fotografias

33. out of focus
fora de foco

34. overexposed
superexposto

35. underexposed
subexposto

A. record
gravar

B. play
rodar / passar

C. fast forward
avançar

D. rewind
rebobinar / voltar

E. pause
dar pausa / congelar a cena

F. stop and **eject**
parar e ejetar

165

Types of entertainment Tipos de entretenimento

1. film / movie
o filme

2. play
a peça de teatro

3. television program
o programa de televisão

4. radio program
o programa de rádio

5. stand-up comedy
o show de comediante

6. concert
o concerto

7. ballet
o balé

8. opera
a ópera

Types of stories Tipos de estórias / gêneros

9. western
o faroeste

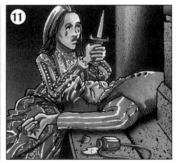

10. comedy
a comédia

11. tragedy
a tragédia

12. science fiction story
a estória de ficção
científica

13. action story /
adventure story
a estória de aventura /
ação

14. horror story
a estória de terror

15. mystery
o mistério / o policial

16. romance
o romance

Types of TV programs   Tipos de programas de TV

17. news
o noticiário

18. sitcom (situation comedy)
o programa de humor

19. cartoon
o desenho-animado

20. talk show
o programa de entrevista

21. soap opera
a novela

22. nature program
o programa sobre a natureza

23. game show/quiz show
o programa de competição

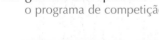

24. children's program
o programa infantil

25. shopping program
o programa de compras pela TV

26. serious book
o livro **sério**

27. funny book
o livro **engraçado**

28. sad book
o livro **triste**

29. boring book
o livro **entediante**

30. interesting book
o livro **interessante**

1. **New Year's Day**
   o Dia de Ano Novo

2. **parade**
   o desfile

3. **confetti**
   confete

4. **Valentine's Day**
   o Dia dos Namorados

5. **card**
   o cartão

6. **heart**
   o coração

7. **Independence Day / 4th of July**
   o Dia da Independência / 4 de julho

8. **fireworks**
   os fogos de artifício

9. **flag**
   a bandeira

10. **Halloween**
    o Dia de Halloween
    (Dia das Bruxas)

11. **jack-o'-lantern**
    a lanterna feita de abóbora

12. **mask**
    a máscara

13. **costume**
    a fantasia

14. **candy**
    os doces

15. **Thanksgiving**
    o Dia de Ação de Graças

16. **feast**
    a celebração / o banquete

17. **turkey**
    o peru

18. **Christmas**
    o Natal

19. **ornament**
    a decoração natalina

20. **Christmas tree**
    a árvore de Natal

A. **plan** a party
   planejar uma festa

B. **invite** the guests
   convidar as pessoas

C. **decorate** the house
   decorar a casa

D. **wrap** a gift
   embrulhar um presente

E. **hide**
   esconder-se

F. **answer** the door
   atender à porta

G. **shout** "surprise!"
   gritar "surpresa"!

H. **light** the candles
   acender as velas

I. **sing** "Happy Birthday"
   cantar "Parabéns a você"

J. **make** a wish
   fazer um pedido

K. **blow out** the candles
   soprar / apagar as velas

L. **open** the presents
   abrir os presentes

Practice inviting friends to a party.

I'd love for you to come to my party <u>next week</u>.

Could <u>you and your friend</u> come to my party?

Would <u>your friend</u> like to come to a party I'm giving?

Share your answers.

1. Do you celebrate birthdays? What do you do?
2. Are there birthdays you celebrate in a special way?
3. Is there a special birthday song in your country?

Verb Guide

Verbs in English are either regular or irregular in the past tense and past participle forms.

Regular Verbs

The regular verbs below are marked 1, 2, 3, or 4 according to four different spelling patterns. (See page 172 for the **irregular verbs** which do not follow any of these patterns.)

Spelling Patterns for the Past and the Past Participle	*Example*		
1. Add **-ed** to the end of the verb.	**ASK**	→	**ASKED**
2. Add **-d** to the end of the verb.	**LIVE**	→	**LIVED**
3. Double the final consonant and add **-ed** to the end of the verb.	**DROP**	→	**DROPPED**
4. Drop the final y and add **-ied** to the end of the verb.	**CRY**	→	**CRIED**

The Oxford Picture Dictionary List of Regular Verbs

act (1)
add (1)
address (1)
answer (1)
apologize (2)
appear (1)
applaud (1)
arrange (2)
arrest (1)
arrive (2)
ask (1)
assemble (2)
assist (1)
bake (2)
barbecue (2)
bathe (2)
board (1)
boil (1)
borrow (1)
bounce (2)
brainstorm (1)
breathe (2)
broil (1)
brush (1)
burn (1)
call (1)
carry (4)
change (2)
check (1)
choke (2)
chop (3)
circle (2)
claim (1)
clap (3)
clean (1)
clear (1)
climb (1)
close (2)
collate (2)

collect (1)
color (1)
comb (1)
commit (3)
compliment (1)
conserve (2)
convert (1)
cook (1)
copy (4)
correct (1)
cough (1)
count (1)
cross (1)
cry (4)
dance (2)
design (1)
deposit (1)
deliver (1)
dial (1)
dictate (2)
die (2)
discuss (1)
dive (2)
dress (1)
dribble (2)
drill (1)
drop (3)
drown (1)
dry (4)
dust (1)
dye (2)
edit (1)
eject (1)
empty (4)
end (1)
enter (1)
erase (2)
examine (2)
exchange (2)

exercise (2)
experience (2)
exterminate (2)
fasten (1)
fax (1)
file (2)
fill (1)
finish (1)
fix (1)
floss (1)
fold (1)
fry (4)
gargle (2)
graduate (2)
grate (2)
grease (2)
greet (1)
grill (1)
hail (1)
hammer (1)
harvest (1)
help (1)
hire (2)
hug (3)
immigrate (2)
inquire (2)
insert (1)
introduce (2)
invite (2)
iron (1)
jog (3)
join (1)
jump (1)
kick (1)
kiss (1)
knit (3)
land (1)
laugh (1)
learn (1)

lengthen (1)
listen (1)
live (2)
load (1)
lock (1)
look (1)
mail (1)
manufacture (2)
mark (1)
match (1)
measure (2)
milk (1)
miss (1)
mix (1)
mop (3)
move (2)
mow (1)
need (1)
nurse (2)
obey (1)
observe (2)
open (1)
operate (2)
order (1)
overdose (2)
paint (1)
park (1)
pass (1)
pause (2)
peel (1)
perm (1)
pick (1)
pitch (1)
plan (3)
plant (1)
play (1)
point (1)
polish (1)
pour (1)
pretend (1)
print (1)
protect (1)

pull (1)
push (1)
race (2)
raise (2)
rake (2)
receive (2)
record (1)
recycle (2)
register (1)
relax (1)
remove (2)
rent (1)
repair (1)
repeat (1)
report (1)
request (1)
return (1)
rinse (2)
roast (1)
rock (1)
sauté (2)
save (2)
scrub (3)
seat (1)
sentence (2)
serve (2)
share (2)
shave (2)
ship (3)
shop (3)
shorten (1)
shout (1)
sign (1)
simmer (1)
skate (2)
ski (1)
slice (2)
smell (1)
sneeze (2)
sort (1)
spell (1)
staple (2)

start (1)
stay (1)
steam (1)
stir (3)
stir-fry (4)
stop (3)
stow (1)
stretch (1)
supervise (2)
swallow (1)
tackle (2)
talk (1)
taste (2)
thank (1)
tie (2)
touch (1)
transcribe (2)
transfer (3)
travel (1)
trim (3)
turn (1)
type (2)
underline (2)
unload (1)
unpack (1)
use (2)
vacuum (1)
vomit (1)
vote (2)
wait (1)
walk (1)
wash (1)
watch (1)
water (1)
weed (1)
weigh (1)
wipe (2)
work (1)
wrap (3)
yield (1)

Irregular Verbs

These verbs have irregular endings in the past and/or the past participle.

The Oxford Picture Dictionary List of Irregular Verbs

simple	past	past participle	simple	past	past participle
be	was	been	leave	left	left
beat	beat	beaten	lend	lent	lent
become	became	become	let	let	let
begin	began	begun	light	lit	lit
bend	bent	bent	make	made	made
bleed	bled	bled	pay	paid	paid
blow	blew	blown	picnic	picnicked	picnicked
break	broke	broken	put	put	put
build	built	built	read	read	read
buy	bought	bought	rewind	rewound	rewound
catch	caught	caught	rewrite	rewrote	rewritten
come	came	come	ride	rode	ridden
cut	cut	cut	run	ran	run
do	did	done	say	said	said
draw	drew	drawn	see	saw	seen
drink	drank	drunk	sell	sold	sold
drive	drove	driven	send	sent	sent
eat	ate	eaten	set	set	set
fall	fell	fallen	sew	sewed	sewn
feed	fed	fed	shoot	shot	shot
feel	felt	felt	sing	sang	sung
find	found	found	sit	sat	sat
fly	flew	flown	speak	spoke	spoken
get	got	gotten	stand	stood	stood
give	gave	given	sweep	swept	swept
go	went	gone	swim	swam	swum
hang	hung	hung	swing	swung	swung
have	had	had	take	took	taken
hear	heard	heard	teach	taught	taught
hide	hid	hidden	throw	threw	thrown
hit	hit	hit	wake	woke	woken
hold	held	held	wear	wore	worn
keep	kept	kept	withdraw	withdrew	withdrawn
lay	laid	laid	write	wrote	written

Index

Two numbers are shown after words in the index: the first refers to the page where the word is illustrated and the second refers to the item number of the word on that page. For example, cool [kōol] **10**-3 means that the word *cool* is item number 3 on page 10. If only the bold page number appears, then that word is part of the unit title or subtitle, or is found somewhere else on the page. A bold number followed by ✦ means the word can be found in the exercise space at the bottom of that page.

Words or combinations of words that appear in **bold** type are used as verbs or verb phrases. Words used as other parts of speech are shown in ordinary type. So, for example, **file** (in bold type) is the verb *file*, while file (in ordinary type) is the noun *file*. Words or phrases in small capital letters (for example, HOLIDAYS) form unit titles.

Phrases and other words that form combinations with an individual word entry are often listed underneath it. Rather than repeating the word each time it occurs in combination with what is listed under it, the word is replaced by three dots (...), called an ellipsis. For example, under the word *bus*, you will find ...driver and ...stop meaning *bus driver* and *bus stop*. Under the word *store* you will find shoe... and toy..., meaning *shoe store* and *toy store*.

Pronunciation Guide

The index includes a pronunciation guide for all the words and phrases illustrated in the book. This guide uses symbols commonly found in dictionaries for native speakers. These symbols, unlike those used in pronunciation systems such as the International Phonetic Alphabet, tend to use English spelling patterns and so should help you to become more aware of the connections between written English and spoken English.

Consonants

[b] as in back [băk]	[k] as in key [kē]	[sh] as in shoe [shōo]
[ch] as in cheek [chēk]	[l] as in leaf [lēf]	[t] as in tape [tāp]
[d] as in date [dāt]	[m] as in match [măch]	[th] as in three [thrē]
[dh] as in this [dhĭs]	[n] as in neck [nĕk]	[v] as in vine [vīn]
[f] as in face [fās]	[ng] as in ring [rĭng]	[w] as in wait [wāt]
[g] as in gas [găs]	[p] as in park [pärk]	[y] as in yams [yămz]
[h] as in half [hăf]	[r] as in rice [rīs]	[z] as in zoo [zōo]
[j] as in jam [jăm]	[s] as in sand [sănd]	[zh] as in measure [mĕzhʹər]

Vowels

[ā] as in bake [bāk]	[ĭ] as in lip [lĭp]	[ow] as in cow [kow]
[ă] as in back [băk]	[ï] as in near [nïr]	[oy] as in boy [boy]
[ä] as in car [kär] or box [bäks]	[ō] as in cold [kōld]	[ŭ] as in cut [kŭt]
[ē] as in beat [bēt]	[ö] as in short [shört]	[ü] as in curb [kürb]
[ĕ] as in bed [bĕd]	or claw [klö]	[ə] as in above [ə bŭvʹ]
[ë] as in bear [bër]	[ōo] as in cool [kōol]	
[ī] as in line [līn]	[ŏo] as in cook [kŏok]	

All the pronunciation symbols used are alphabetical except for the schwa [ə]. The schwa is the most frequent vowel sound in English. If you use the schwa appropriately in unstressed syllables, your pronunciation will sound more natural.

Vowels before [r] are shown with the symbol [¨] to call attention to the special quality that vowels have before [r]. (Note that the symbols [ä] and [ö] are also used for vowels not followed by [r], as in *box* or *claw*.) You should listen carefully to native speakers to discover how these vowels actually sound.

Stress

This index follows the system for marking stress used in many dictionaries for native speakers.

1. Stress is not marked if a word consisting of a single syllable occurs by itself.

2. Where stress is marked, two levels are distinguished:

a bold accent [ʹ] is placed after each syllable with primary (or strong) stress, a light accent [ʹ] is placed after each syllable with secondary (or weaker) stress.

In phrases and other combinations of words, stress is indicated for each word as it would be pronounced within the whole phrase or other unit. If a word consisting of a single syllable is stressed in the combinations listed below it, the accent mark indicating the degree of stress it has in the phrases (primary or secondary) is shown in parentheses. A hyphen replaces any part of a word or phrase that is omitted. For example, bus [bŭs(ʹ–)] shows that the word *bus* is said with primary stress in the combinations shown below it. The word ...driver [–drīʹvər], listed under *bus*, shows that *driver* has secondary stress in the combination *bus driver*: [bŭsʹ drīʹvər]

Syllable Boundaries

Syllable boundaries are indicated by a single space or by a stress mark.

Note: The pronunciations shown in this index are based on patterns of American English. There has been no attempt to represent all of the varieties of American English. Students should listen to native speakers to hear how the language actually sounds in a particular region.

Index

Index

Index

Index

Index

Index

Index

Index

Index

Index

Index

Geographical Index

Continents

Countries and other locations

Bodies of water

The United States of America

Regions of the United States

Geographical Index

States of the United States
Alabama [ăl/ə băm/ə] **122–123**
Alaska [ə lăs/kə] **122–125**
Arizona [ăr/ə zō/nə] **122–123**
Arkansas [är/kən sö/] **122–123**
California [kăl/ə förn/yə] **122–123**
Colorado [kăl/ə răd/ō, –ra/dō] **122–123**
Connecticut [kə nĕt/ĭ kət] **122–123**
Delaware [dĕl/ə wĕr/] **122–123**
Florida [flör/ə də, flär/–] **122–123**
Georgia [jör/jə] **122–123**
Hawaii [hə wī/ē] **122–123**
Idaho [ī/də hō/] **122–123**
Illinois [ĭl/ə noy/] **122–123**
Indiana [ĭn/dē ăn/ə] **122–123**
Iowa [ī/ə wə] **122–123**
Kansas [kăn/zəs] **122–123**
Kentucky [kən tŭk/ē] **122–123**
Louisiana [lōō ē/zē ăn/ə] **122–123**
Maine [mān] **122–123**
Maryland [mĕr/ə lənd] **122–123**
Massachusetts [măs/ə chōō/səts] **122–123**
Michigan [mĭsh/ĭ gən] **122–123**
Minnesota [mĭn/ə sō/tə] **122–123**
Mississippi [mĭs/ə sĭp/ē] **122–123**
Missouri [mə zōōr/ē, –zōōr/ə] **122–123**
Montana [män tăn/ə] **122–123**
Nebraska [nə brăs/kə] **122–123**
Nevada [nə văd/ə, –vä/də] **122–123**
New Hampshire [nōō/ hămp/shər] **122–123**
New Jersey [nōō/ jür/zē] **122–123**
New Mexico [nōō/ mĕk/sĭ kō/] **122–123**
New York [nōō/ yörk/] **122–123**
North Carolina [nörth/ kăr/ə lī/nə] **122–123**
North Dakota [nörth/ də kō/tə] **122–123**
Ohio [ō hī/ō] **122–123**
Oklahoma [ō/klə hō/mə] **122–123**
Oregon [ör/ĭ gən, –gän/, är/–] **122–123**
Pennsylvania [pĕn/səl vän/yə] **122–123**
Rhode Island [rōd/ ī/lənd] **122–123**
South Carolina [sowth/ kăr/ə lī/nə] **122–123**
South Dakota [sowth/ də kō/tə] **122–123**
Tennessee [tĕn/ə sē/] **122–123**
Texas [tĕk/səs] **122–123**
Utah [yōō/tö, –tä] **122–123**
Vermont [vər mänt/] **122–123**
Virginia [vər jĭn/yə] **122–123**
Washington [wä/shĭng tən, wö/–] **122–123**
West Virginia [wĕst/ vər jĭn/yə] **122–123**
Wisconsin [wĭs kän/sən] **122–123**
Wyoming [wī ō/mĭng] **122–123**

Canada
Capital: Ottawa [ät/ə wə]

Regions of Canada
Atlantic Provinces [ət lăn/tĭk präv/ən səz] **123**–6
British Columbia [brĭt/ĭsh kə lŭm/bē ə] **123**–2
Northern Canada [nör/dhərn kăn/ə də] **123**–1
Ontario [än tër/ē ō/] **123**–4
Prairie Provinces [prĕ/ē präv/ən səz] **123**–3
Quebec [kwĭ bĕk/] **123**–5

Provinces of Canada
Alberta [ăl bür/tə] **122–123**
British Columbia [brĭt/ĭsh kə lŭm/bē ə] **122–123**
Manitoba [măn/ə tō/bə] **122–123**

New Brunswick [nōō/ brŭnz/wĭk] **122–123**
Newfoundland [nōō/fən lənd] **122–123**
Northwest Territories [nörth/wĕst/ tĕr/ə tör/ēz] **122–123**
Nova Scotia [nō/və skō/shə] **122–123**
Ontario [än tër/ē ō/] **122–123**
Prince Edward Island [prĭns/ ĕd/wərd ī/lənd] **122–123**
Quebec [kwĭ bĕk/] **122–123**
Saskatchewan [să skăch/ə wən, –wän/] **122–123**
Yukon Territory [yōō/kän tĕr/ə tör/ē] **122–123**

Mexico
Capital: Mexico (City) [mĕk/sĭ kō/ (sĭt/ē)]

Regions of Mexico
Chiapas Highlands [chē ä/pəs hī/ləndz] **123**–18
Gulf Coastal Plain [gŭlf/ kō/stəl plān/] **123**–16
Pacific Northwest [pə sĭf/ĭk nörth/wĕst] **123**–14
Plateau of Mexico [plă tō/ əv mĕk/sĭ kō/] **123**–15
Southern Uplands [sŭdh/ərn ŭp/ləndz] **123**–17
Yucatan Peninsula [yōō/kə tăn/ pə nĭn/sə lə, yōō/kə tän/–] **123**–19

States of Mexico
Aguascalientes [ä/gwəs käl yĕn/tās] **122–123**
Baja California Norte [bä/hä kăl/ə förn/yə nör/tā] **122–123**
Baja California Sur [bä/hä kăl/ə förn/yə sōōr/] **122–123**
Campeche [käm pā/chä, käm pē/chē] **122–123**
Chiapas [chē ä/pəs] **122–123**
Chihuahua [chĭ wä/wä, –wə] **122–123**
Coahuila [kō/ə wē/lə] **122–123**
Colima [kə lē/mə] **122–123**
Distrito Federal [dĭ strē/tō fĕd/ə räl/] **122–123**
Durango [dŏŏ răng/yō, –räng/–] **122–123**
Guanajuato [gwä/nə hwä/tō] **122–123**
Guerrero [gə rër/ō] **122–123**
Hidalgo [hĭ däl/gō, ē dhäl/gō] **122–123**
Jalisco [hə lĭs/kō, –lēs/–] **122–123**
México [mĕk/sĭ kō/, mĕ/hē kō] **122–123**
Michoacán [mē/chō ä kän/] **122–123**
Morelos [mö rĕl/ōs] **122–123**
Nayarit [nä/yə rēt/] **122–123**
Nuevo León [nwā/vō lā ōn/] **122–123**
Oaxaca [wə hä/kə, wä–] **122–123**
Puebla [pwĕb/lä] **122–123**
Querétaro [kə rĕt/ə rō/] **122–123**
Quintana Roo [kēn tä/nə rō/] **122–123**
San Luis Potosí [sän/ lōō ēs/ pō/tə sē/] **122–123**
Sinaloa [sē/nə lō/ə] **122–123**
Sonora [sə nör/ə] **122–123**
Tabasco [tə băs/kō] **122–123**
Tamaulipas [tä/mow lē/pəs] **122–123**
Tlaxcala [tlä skä/lə] **122–123**
Veracruz [vĕr/ə krōōz/, –krōōs/] **122–123**
Yucatán [yōō/kə tän/, –tän/] **122–123**
Zacatecas [zä/kə tä/kəs, sä/–] **122–123**